WELDING

BASICS

An Introduction to Practical & Ornamental Welding

CREATIVE
PUBLISHING
international

CHANHASSEN, MINNESOTA

www.creativepub.com

CONTENTS

Printed by R. R. Donnelley
10 9 8 7 6 5 4 3 2 1

President/CEO: *Michael Eleftheriou*
Vice President/Publisher: *Linda Ball*
Vice President/Retail Sales & Marketing: *Kevin Haas*

Executive Editor: *Bryan Trandem*
Creative Director: *Tim Himsel*
Managing Editor: *Michelle Skudlarek*
Editorial Director: *Jerri Farris*

Author: *Karen Ruth*
Art Director: *Kari Johnston*
Copy Editor: *Brett Martin*
Project Manager: *Tracy Stanley*
Technical Editor: *Dwight Affeldt*
Proofreader: *Linnéa Christensen*
Illustrator: *Earl Slack*
Photo Researcher: *Julie Caruso*
Studio Services Manager: *Jeanette Moss McCurdy*
Photo Team Leader: *Tate Carlson*
Photographer: *Joel Schnell*
Scene Shop Carpenter: *Randy Austin*
Scene Shop Assistant: *Jacob Austin*
Director of Production Services & Photography: *Kim Gerber*
Production Manager: *Helga Thielen*

Welding Basics: An Introduction to Practical & Ornamental Welding
Created by: The Editors of Creative Publishing international, Inc.

Other titles from Creative Publishing international include:
The New Everyday Home Repairs; Basic Wiring & Electrical Repairs; Building Decks; Home Masonry Projects & Repairs; Workshop Tips & Techniques; Bathroom Remodeling; Flooring Projects & Techniques; Decorative Accessories; Kitchen Accessories; Maximizing Minimal Space; Outdoor Wood Furnishings; Easy Wood Furniture Projects; Customizing Your Home; Carpentry: Remodeling; Carpentry: Tools • Shelves • Walls • Doors; Exterior Home Repairs & Improvements; Home Plumbing Projects & Repairs; Advanced Home Wiring; Advanced Deck Building; Built-In Projects for the Home; Landscape Design & Construction; Refinishing & Finishing Wood; Building Porches & Patios; Advanced Home Plumbing; Remodeling Kitchens; Finishing Basements & Attics; Stonework & Masonry Projects; Sheds, Gazebos & Outbuildings; Building & Finishing Walls & Ceilings; Customizing Your Home; The Complete Guide to Home Plumbing; The Complete Guide to Home Wiring; The Complete Guide to Building Decks; The Complete Guide to Painting & Decorating; The Complete Guide to Creative Landscapes; The Complete Guide to Home Masonry; The Complete Guide to Home Carpentry; The Complete Guide to Home Storage; The Complete Guide to Windows & Doors; The Complete Guide to Bathrooms; The Complete Guide to Easy Woodworking Projects; The Complete Guide to Flooring; The Complete Guide to Ceramic & Stone Tile; The Complete Photo Guide to Home Repair; The Complete Photo Guide to Home Improvement; The Complete Photo Guide to Outdoor Home Improvement; Accessible Home; Open House; Lighting Design & Installation.

Library of Congress
Cataloging-in-Publication Data
Welding basics : an introduction to practical & ornamental welding.
   p. cm.
   ISBN 1-58923-139-2 (sc.)
   1. Welding. I. Creative Publishing International.
TS227.W355 2003
671.5'2--dc22   2003055399

A simple flame-cut silhouette is a charming addition to any garden.

INTRODUCTION

Welding is a practical skill that is also great fun. The number of welded items in our everyday lives is practically uncountable—the spot welds on the bodies of our automobile, the welded railing on our front steps, the superstructure of the buildings in which we work, and the bridges over which we drive. But welding also makes smaller, more delicate functional and decorative items possible, like patio chairs and trellises, wine racks and candleholders, baker's shelves and headboards. The photos on these pages reveal only a fraction of what welding artisans have created with heat and metal.

The costs involved in setting up a well-equipped home welding shop are comparable to setting up a well-equipped woodworking shop. A great advantage of welding is that the materials are generally inexpensive, yet you can create items that sell in shops for hundreds of dollars. Because fewer people are knowledgeable about welding, there is always a rewarding "awe" factor to showing off what you have created.

This book provides basic directions and step-by-step photos that illustrate the four major welding processes and the two major cutting processes. You also

©Millet/Inside/Beateworks

The strength and malleability of steel makes it perfectly suitable for forming whimsical structures like this candelabra.

Photo courtesy of Sleeper Welding/Tom Sleeper. Opposite photo/©John Gregor

Cutting and welding creates beautiful and useful household items, like this fireplace screen.

A variety of metals, shapes, and joining techniques were combined to create this beautiful artwork.

will find quick reference charts that describe electrode and filler wire choices, metals and their weldability, and joint and weld types. Suggestions for setting up a welding shop, detailed safety guidelines, and ideas for finishing your metal projects are also included.

Best of all, this book includes detailed directions for 23 practical and decorative projects. You can make a welding and cutting table for your welding shop, a scrolled desktop lamp, a wrought iron railing, or a cute critter boot brush. You can practice your techniques and make accessories for your own home or as gifts. We also encourage you to use the project ideas to branch out and create your own versions of a baker's rack, coffee table, or kitchen accessory stand.

These colorful puppies are cut from junked car hoods.

Creating fanciful creatures from garden tools is a rewarding welding project.

Simple and graceful arches and trellises are easily made from mild steel. A few bends, decorative finials, and a handful of welds are all it took to make this simple garden archway.

(above left) Scales of sheet metal, springy legs, and mesh trolleys— what a fun piggy collection.

(above right) Old tools and recycled metal odds and ends make this gate geometrically pleasing.

(middle left) Old farm implements and spare parts are great sources of weldable material. This chicken shows what a little imagination can do with a pile of parts.

(middle right) The strength of steel allows for solid yet airy structures like this plant stand.

NOTICE TO READERS:

Welding is a dangerous activity. Failure to follow safety procedures may result in serious injury or death. This book provides useful instruction, but we cannot anticipate all of your working conditions or the characteristics of your materials and tools. For safety, you should use caution, care, and good judgment when following the procedures described in this book. Consider your own skill level and the instructions and safety precautions associated with the various tools and materials shown. The publisher cannot assume responsibility for any damage to property or injury to persons as a result of misuse of the information provided.

Oxyacetylene welding

Shielded metal arc welding

Gas metal arc welding

Introduction to Welding

Welding is all about heat, about using heat to melt separate pieces of metal so they will flow together and fuse to form a single, seamless piece. Regardless of the welding or cutting process, your ability to control the heat generated by the flame or arc determines the quality of your welds and cuts.

Certain terms are used to describe the heat and action of all the welding processes. The parts being welded together are referred to as the base metal. Additional metal, called filler, is often added to the weld. The molten puddle is the area of melted base metal and filler metal that you maintain as you create your weld. To have fusion of metals, the base metal and filler metals must be the same composition. Methods for joining metal without fusion are called soldering, brazing, and braze welding. These methods can be used to join similar or dissimilar metals.

Oxyacetylene welding and cutting use flames to generate the heat to melt the metal. Shielded metal arc, gas metal arc, and gas tungsten arc welding and plasma cutting use an electric arc for heat generation. With oxyacetylene welding, you have time to watch the puddle develop as the metal turns red, then glossy and wet looking, then finally melts. With the arc processes, the puddle forms quickly and may be difficult to see because of the intensity of the arc. It is important to have ample lighting and clear vision so you can watch the puddle and move it steadily.

Penetration of the weld is also a critical heat dependent factor. A strong weld penetrates all the way through the base metal. Matching filler material size and heat input to the thickness of the base metal is important. It is easy to get a good looking weld that has not penetrated the base metal at all and merely sits on the surface. At the opposite end of the spectrum from a "cold," non-penetrating weld is burn through—where the base metal has gotten too hot and is entirely burned away, leaving a hole in the base metal and the weld.

Heat distortion is a by-product of all welding and cutting processes. It is obvious that applying a flame to metal in the oxyacetylene process makes the metal hot—and the electrical arcs are actually four to five thousand degrees hotter than the oxyacetylene flame.

When metal is heated it expands; when it cools it contracts. If not taken into consideration, this expansion and contraction may cause parts to move out of alignment. This is why tack welding and clamping project pieces is critical to successful welding. It is also important to match the welding process to the base metal thickness. For example, shielded metal arc welding is generally not used on materials less than ⅛" thick. The process is too hot and too difficult to control on thin material. On the other hand, gas metal arc welding works well on very thin sheet metal, if you are able to adjust the machine to a low enough voltage.

Protecting the molten puddle from oxygen is also an important part of welding. Oxygen makes steel rust and causes corrosion in other metals. The exclusion of oxygen from the weld when it is in the molten state makes a stronger weld. This is accomplished in a variety of ways. A properly adjusted oxyacetylene flame burns off the ambient oxygen in a small zone around the weld puddle. Gas metal arc and gas tungsten arc welding bathe the weld in an inert gas from a pressurized cylinder. These inert gases keep oxygen away from the molten puddle. Flux cored arc welding and shielded metal arc welding use fluxes in or on the welding filler metal. When these fluxes burn, they produce shielding gases and slag, both of which protect the weld area until it has cooled.

Welding well is difficult and takes years to master, but it is possible to make many useful and decorative items with basic knowledge and a little practice. If you wish to move beyond the decorative projects outlined in this book, it is a good idea to talk with a welder and have him or her evaluate some of your welds. Remember, the safety of others is involved when you choose to make a utility trailer or spiral staircase. Take the time and make the effort to ensure that any structural project you make is safe.

This book is intended as a reference for people who have had some exposure to welding and need reminders about what steps to follow and precautions to take. It is not intended to teach welding to someone who has never handled welding equipment. Many community colleges, technical schools, and art centers offer welding classes. Such classes are an ideal way to learn the basics of welding, proper techniques for each process, and welding safety.

Gas tungsten arc welding

Plasma cutting

Oxyacetylene cutting

Welding safety includes protecting yourself with protective gear, following manufacturer's instructions, and being aware of the surroundings in which you are welding.

Safety

Welding can be a dangerous activity. Possibilities exist for getting cut, burned, electrocuted, and causing fires or explosions. Preparations for welding—grinding, burnishing, and sawing—are also dangerous. That said, it is absolutely possible, with a little care and diligence, to weld for years and never suffer more than a burnt thumb from being too eager to examine a just-completed weld.

It is very important to follow manufacturer's specific instructions and recommendations for equipment and product use and to follow general welding safety rules. Whether you are welding in a dedicated welding shop or have set up your own shop at home, you need to be aware of a number of specific safety concerns.

Fumes. Welding produces hazardous smoke and fumes. It is always important to keep your face out of the weld plume. Welding indoors requires either a ventilation fan, exhaust hood, or fume extractor. Wear an OSHA approved N99 particle mask or a respirator. If you are pregnant or plan to become pregnant, a respirator is a necessity.

Burns. Hot sparks and flying slag can cause burns. Protect your hands, head, and body with natural fibers—leather, wool, or cotton. Manufactured fibers such as nylon and polyester melt when ignited, which causes serious burns. Wear leather slip-on boots, and make sure your pant legs fall over the top of your footwear. Cuffed pants and pants with frayed edges are fire hazards. Also, welding sparks will find tiny holes, so don't wear holey jeans. Wear a welding cap and tie back long hair and keep it tucked under your shirt or cap.

Arc burn. Welding arcs produce ultraviolet and infrared light. Both of these can damage your eyes permanently, burn your skin, and potentially lead to skin cancer. A welding helmet with a filter lens protects your eyes and face, while long sleeve shirts and long pants protect your skin. Remember, you are also responsible for protecting the vision of curious neighbors, passersby, and pets. Use welding screens and have an extra helmet on hand for observers.

Fire. The area you're working in should be cleared of any flammable items such as lumber, rags, dropcloths, cigarette lighters, and matches. Absolutely do not weld or grind metal in a sawdust-filled shop. Sparks from welding and grinding can ignite airborne dust or fumes, or travel across the floor and come to rest against flammable materials. A fire extinguisher rated ABC is a must—mount it next to a first aid kit so you know where both are. Check your welding area one half hour after welding to make sure no sparks have found a place to smolder.

Explosion. Even non-flammable gases such as carbon dioxide are stored in cylinders at such high pressure that they can easily become dangerous missiles. Keep the cylinder's protective cap on if regulators are not installed, and keep cylinders chained or strapped at all times. Cylinders should never be used as rollers or supports, and cylinders and protective caps should never be welded on. Shut acetylene and oxygen cylinder valves if you're away for more than 10 minutes. Cylinders must be transported right side up and chained, even if empty.

Another explosion hazard is concrete. Because of the amount of water contained in concrete, it can become a steam bomb if welded upon. Tack welding on concrete is acceptable, but using a concrete surface to back your welds is not. Use fire bricks, which have been cured to have very low water content. Never weld or cut on any closed container, tank, or cylinder. Even if it has been empty for years, it might have enough residual material to release toxic fumes or explode. Always bring tanks of any sort to a tank welding specialist for repair.

Other hazards include noise from grinding, sawing, sanding, and plasma cutting; laceration from sharp metal edges; electrocution during arc welding; and asphyxiation from inert shielding gases. Carefully read all manufacturers' instructions before starting any welding process.

MINIMUM LENS SHADE NUMBERS FOR WELDING

APPLICATION	SUGGESTED SHADE #
Shielded Metal Arc Welding (SMAW)	
1/16 to 5/32" electrodes	10
3/16 to 1/4" electrodes	12
5/16 to 3/8" electrodes	14
Gas Metal Arc Welding (GMAW)	
1/16 to 5/32" non-ferrous	11
1/16 to 5/32" ferrous	12
Gas Tungsten Arc Welding (GTAW)	10 to 14
Plasma Cutting	8
Oxyacetylene Welding	5
Oxyacetylene Cutting	5
Brazing	3 to 5

Welding helmets are typically available with filter lenses in either 2" × 4¼" or 4½" × 5¼" sizes. Helmets with auto-darkening lenses are also available. Full-face protective shields are available in clear, for grinding or chipping, and with a #5 filter for oxyacetylene operations.

Welding safety equipment includes: A. safety glasses, B. particle mask, C. low-profile respirator, D. leather slip-on boots, E. fire-retardant jacket, F. fire-retardant jacket with leather sleeves, G. welding cap, H. leather cape with apron, I. leather gloves with gauntlets, J. heavy-duty welding gloves, K. welding helmet with auto-darkening lens, L. welding helmet with flip-up lens, M. full-face #5 filter, N. full-face clear protective shield.

Shop space with a concrete floor and cement block walls is ideal for welding. Good ventilation is also important.

Setting Up Shop

If you plan to weld on a regular basis, it makes sense to set up a welding shop. The primary concern with welding is containing the hot sparks or slag and the flammable elements while exhausting dangerous fumes. It is possible to weld outside, but not all processes allow that. Gas metal and gas tungsten arc welding require that the surrounding air be still so the shielding gas is not disturbed. All the arc processes must be done in dry conditions to prevent electrical shock. Cold metals do not respond as well as metals at 70° F and may not be weldable using certain processes. A heated garage or outbuilding is best suited for a welding shop. A basement is not suitable due to the dangers of fire and compressed gases next to living spaces. Additionally, your homeowner's insurance may not cover a welding shop if it is inside your living area as opposed to in a detached garage or shop building.

It is important to remember that tiny sparks and pieces of hot slag may scatter up to 30 or 40 feet from the source. If they come to rest on flammable materials, they may smolder, and given the right conditions, can ignite the material. Always check your welding area one half hour after you have completed welding to make certain no sparks are smoldering. A wooden table covered with metal is not a good work surface, as the transferred heat may cause the wood to smolder. Any wooden jigs or clamping devices should be doused with water to extinguish smoldering embers or stored outside after use.

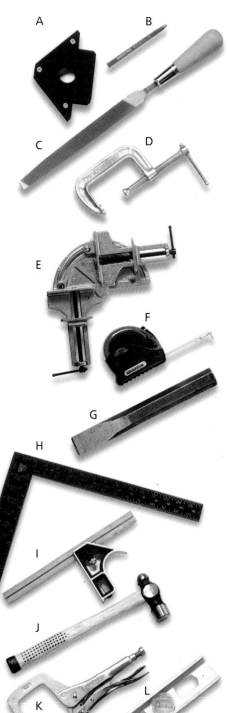

Shop Tools

Power tools such as the reciprocating saw, angle grinder, portable band saw, and chop saw are useful when cutting and fitting metal parts to be welded. A drill press and metal cutting band saw are also useful tools for welding.

Specific metal working tools, including metal brakes and metal benders, are available for all sizes of metal. These can range from inexpensive sheet metal tools, such as the scroll bender shown on page 108, to expensive hydraulic tools.

Standard tools for a welding shop (right photo) include: A. magnetic clamp, B. center punch, C. metal file, D. C-clamp, E. corner clamp, F. tape measure, G. cold chisel, H. carpenter's square, I. combination square, J. ball peen hammer, K. clamping pliers, L. magnetic level, M. hacksaw.

Power tools for a welding shop (above photo) include: A. reciprocating saw, B. chop saw, C. portable band saw, D. angle grinder.

Brass

Copper

Galvanized steel

Mild steel

Metal Basics

Weldability & Cutability

Different metals have different characteristics that affect their ability to be welded or cut with any of the processes described in this book. In general, only metals of the same type are welded together because welding involves melting the base metal parts and adding melted filler metal. In order to accomplish this, the parts and filler must have the same melting temperature and characteristics. Dissimilar metals can be joined by brazing and braze welding because these processes do not actually melt the base metal.

Metals are divided into the categories of ferrous and non-ferrous. Ferrous metals contain iron and will generally be attracted to a magnet. Cast iron, forged steel, mild steel, and stainless steel all contain iron, along with varying amounts of carbon and other alloying elements.

Mild steel, which has a low carbon content, is the most commonly used type of steel and the easiest with which to work. Mild steel can be welded with all the processes covered in this book and can be cut with either oxyfuel or plasma cutting. It makes up most of the metal items you commonly use, make, or repair,

METAL	WELDING PROCESS	CUTTING PROCESS
Mild steel	All welding processes	Oxyfuel, plasma
Aluminum	Gas tungsten arc, gas metal arc	Plasma
Stainless steel	Gas tungsten arc, gas metal arc, shielded metal arc	Plasma
Chrome moly steel	Gas tungsten arc, oxyfuel	Plasma
Titanium	Gas tungsten arc	Plasma
Cast iron	Shielded metal arc, brazing	Plasma
Brass	Braze welding	Plasma

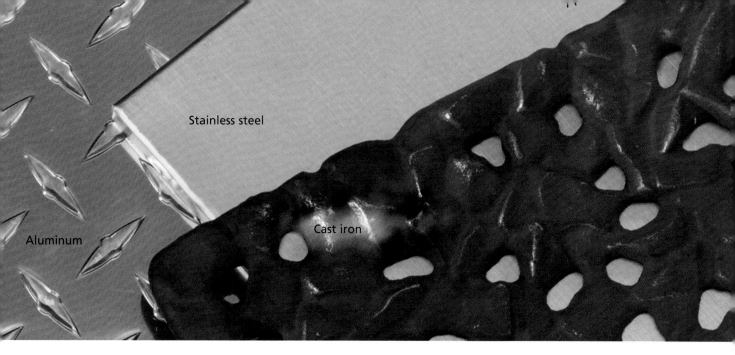

Stainless steel

Cast iron

Aluminum

METAL MELTING POINTS

METAL	MELTING POINT (F)
Aluminum	1217°
Brass	1652-1724°
Bronze	1566-1832°
Chromium	3034°
Copper	1981°
Gold	1946°
Iron	2786°
Lead	621°
Mild steel	2462-2786°
Titanium	3263°
Tungsten	5432°
Zinc	786°

such as automobile bodies, bicycles, railings, patio furniture, file cabinets, and shelving. Adding more carbon to steel makes it harder, more brittle, and more difficult to cut and weld. High carbon steel is called tool steel and is used to make drill bits and other metal cutting tools.

Other elements are added to steel to make a variety of alloys, such as chrome moly steel and stainless steel. These additions may make the steel non-magnetic. Because stainless steel does not oxidize (rust) easily, it is difficult to cut with oxyfuel. When welding steel alloys, the filler material must be matched to the alloy to get a high-quality weld.

In addition to alloying, many metals are heat-treated to improve characteristics such as hardness. Because welding and cutting would reheat these metals and destroy those characteristics, heat-treating is an important factor to consider. Many vehicle chassis parts, including motorcycles and bicycles, are made of heat-treated metals.

Aluminum is a widely used non-ferrous metal because of its light weight and corrosion resistance. Like steel, it is available in many alloys and is often heat treated. Aluminum is used for engine parts, boats, bicycles, furniture, and kitchenware. Various characteristics make aluminum difficult to weld successfully—it does not change color when it melts, it conducts heat rapidly, and it immediately develops an oxidized layer.

A

B

C

D

E

F

G

H

I

J

Metal Shapes & Sizes

Mild steel (and most other metals) come in a variety of shapes, sizes, and thicknesses. Metal thickness may be given as a fraction of an inch, a decimal, or a gauge (see chart, opposite page).

Rectangular tube (A) and **square tube** (B) are used for structural framing, trailers, and furniture. Dimensions for rectangular and square tubing are given as width × height × wall thickness × length.

Rail cap (C) is used for making handrails. Rail cap dimensions are the overall width and the widths of the channels on the underside.

Channel (D) is often used for making handrails. Very large channel is used for truck bodies. The legs, or flanges, make it stronger than flat bars. Dimensions for channel are given as flange thickness × flange height × channel (outside) height × length.

Round tube (E) is not the same as pipe. Round tube is used for structures, and pipe is used for carrying liquids or gases. Dimensions for round tube are given as outside diameter (O.D.) × wall thickness × length. Pipe dimensions are nominal, that is, in name only. They are given as nominal inside diameter (I.D.) × length.

T-bar (F) dimensions are given as width × height × thickness of flanges × length.

Angle or **angle iron** (G) has many structural and decorative uses. Dimensions for angle iron are flange thickness × flange width × flange height × length.

Square bar (H), **round bar** (I), and **hexagonal** or **hex bar** (J) dimensions are given as width or outside diameter × length.

Flat bar or **strap** (not pictured) is available in many sizes. Dimensions are given as thickness × width × length.

Sheet metal (not pictured) is 3⁄16" or less in thickness and is often referred to by gauge. **Plate metal** is more than 3⁄16" thick and is referred to by fractions or inches.

Purchasing Metal

Finding a metal supplier can be a challenging task. The materials that are readily available may not be the sizes and shapes needed for a project and may be expensive. Metal dealerships may not be friendly to small accounts. Because steel is so heavy, Internet or catalog shopping carries prohibitive shipping costs. With some searching, however, most necessary materials can be found.

Metal is generally priced by weight, unless you are purchasing it at a retail store. The price for small pieces of mild steel at a home center or hardware store work out to be as much as $2 to $3 per pound. The price per pound for small orders at a steel dealership may be in the range of 50 cents. Large orders or repeat orders may be priced as low as 30 cents per pound. Many metal suppliers have an odds and ends bin or rack where pieces may be as low as 10 cents per pound. Specialty metals such as stainless steel and aluminum start at $2 to $3 per pound.

Smaller sizes and shapes of mild steel and aluminum are available at home improvement and hardware stores in three-, four-, and six-foot lengths. Welding supply stores often have a selection of ten- and twelve-foot lengths of the commonly used sizes. Steel dealers have most common sizes in stock and will order other sizes for you. Most mild steel shapes and sizes come in twenty-foot lengths, and many steel dealers will make one free courtesy cut per piece. You might want to have the metal delivered, depending on the amount of material you are purchasing. You can order metal through catalogs or the Internet, but remember that shipping is expensive.

Some steel dealers are distributors for decorative metal products, but many specialty items such as wrought iron railing materials, decorative items, and weldable hardware are only available by catalog. A number of catalog supply houses sell to the public and have varied selections and reasonable prices. (See Resources, page 140.)

INCH EQUIVALENT FOR GAUGE THICKNESS

GAUGE	INCHES
24	0.020
22	0.026
20	0.032
18	0.043
16	0.054
14	0.069
12	0.098
11	0.113
10	0.128

Metal less than ⅛" thick is often referred to by gauge. For reference, the decimal equivalent of ⅛" is 0.125.

Sheet metal is available as pierced or expanded. Wall plates, hooks, rings, balls, bushings, candle cups, drip plates, and stamped or cast items are available in a wide variety of shapes, sizes, and metals.

Cleaning the mill scale off mild steel is an important step. A bench mounted power wire brush works well on small pieces. Wire brushing the entire project prior to finishing is critical for good paint adhesion.

Preparing Metal for Welding

A successful weld begins with a well-prepared piece of metal. The cleaner the pieces to be welded, the better the weld quality and appearance. When working with mild steel, it is possible to clean batches of parts ahead of time. When working with aluminum, parts need to be cleaned immediately before welding due to aluminum's nearly instant formation of a protective layer of oxidation. Mild steel is usually covered with mill scale and, often, oil or grease. Round and square tubes are usually thickly coated with oil, which helps in the manufacturing process. This oil can be removed with denatured alcohol, acetone, or a commercial degreaser.

After the oil has been cleaned off, the mill scale can be removed by wire brushing manually or with a bench-mounted or hand-held power wire brush, with sandpaper or sanding screens, or with an angle or bench grinder. Aluminum and stainless steel need to be brushed with stainless steel brushes that are dedicated to cleaning only that metal. Small particles of mild steel will contaminate aluminum and stainless steel welds.

Finishing Metal

Though most commercially available metal items—patio furniture, indoor furniture, and garden accessories—have rough welds and spatter still present, it is nice to grind these down on your projects. An angle grinder is good for flat area welds, and a small rotary grinding tool can get into nooks and crannies. You'll be pleased with the results of a nicely ground, good weld because it looks like a solid piece of metal. Wire brushing, sanding, or sandblasting the entire piece will further prepare it for finishing.

Painting metal projects is best accomplished by spraying, not brushing. You will need to thoroughly clean all oil, dirt, slag, and spatter from the project because even advanced rusty metal primers will not to stick to dirty, oily areas. Metal spray paints are available in various finishes and a huge array of colors.

Powder coating and brass plating are other, more expensive, finish options. Various antiquing and rusting finishes are available as well, or you can let the piece slowly rust on its own if you prefer this look.

An angle grinder works well for beveling edges on thick material. Grinding down welds gives projects a finished look.

Metal Shaping Techniques

There are a number of ways to bend and shape mild steel. Bending tools for creating right angle bends are called metal brakes. Rollers create circles, punches make holes, and shearers make cuts. You can purchase simple hand-powered metalworking tools, though they can be costly—the higher the quality or larger the capacity, the higher the price. (See page 108 for a photo of a scroll bender.) Powerful hydraulic metal shaping tools made for commercial use can cost thousands of dollars.

Simple bending jigs can be made using any round, rigid, strong form, such as pipe and salvaged flywheels, pulley wheels, or wheel rims. Using these jigs, it is fairly easy to bend round rod up to ¼" in diameter and flat bars up to ⅛" thick into complex shapes. Rebar up to ⅜" can be bent into large curves by clamping it into a bench vise. Tubing can be bent using an electrical conduit bender. Thick material such as rail cap can be heated and bent.

You can bend materials more easily if you have a long end to apply pressure to, so you may want to cut pieces to length *after* bending. Whenever you shape metal into sharp angles, take into account the length needed for the radius of the bend. Also, cold-formed metal will spring back somewhat, so it may take trial and error to find what size jig will make the size bend you desire.

Use a sturdy hacksaw, jig saw, or reciprocating saw with bi-metal blades to saw metal. A miter box will help you make accurate cuts. A metal band saw, either portable or bench mounted, is handy if you will be making many projects that require numerous cuts. You can drill metal with a power drill or drill press, using metal cutting bits and oiling the bit often to prevent overheating. Large holes or holes in very thick material might be made more easily with an oxyfuel cutter or plasma cutter. An angle grinder or bench grinder can be used to create tapers or to correct miscut items to get better fit ups for welding.

Bending jigs can be made from any rigid circular item. An engine flywheel, toilet flange, and various pipe sizes are shown here.

Use a vise style pliers to hold the metal to the jig. Wrap the metal around the jig in a smooth motion.

Use a slower drill speed and a metal cutting bit for metal drilling. Frequent application of oil prevents overheating.

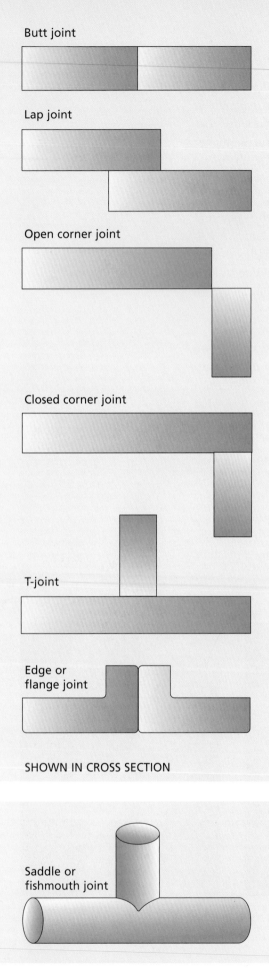

Butt joint

Lap joint

Open corner joint

Closed corner joint

T-joint

Edge or flange joint

SHOWN IN CROSS SECTION

Saddle or fishmouth joint

Joint Types

The basic joints in welding are the butt joint, lap joint, corner joint, T-joint, edge joint, and saddle joint.

The **butt joint** is two pieces in the same plane butted against each other. The gap between the pieces is determined by the thickness of the pieces. Whether or not the surfaces need to be ground down (beveled) is also determined by the plate thickness. The type of weld used for a butt joint is a **groove weld.** The butt joint is a weak joint and should be avoided if at all possible.

A **lap joint** is two pieces in the same plane overlapped. The type of weld used for a lap joint is called a **fillet weld.** The strongest lap joint has welds on both sides.

A **corner joint** is two pieces coming together to make a right angle at a corner. The joint can be open, partially open, or closed. An open corner takes a fillet weld, but other corner joints may take groove welds. For hobby welding on metal ³⁄₁₆" and thinner, an open corner joint is stronger and allows more penetration. A closed corner joint may be weakened if the weld is ground.

A **T-joint** is two pieces placed together to make a right angle T shape. Again, it is welded with a fillet weld. A T-joint is stronger if both sides are welded.

The **edge joint,** or **flange joint,** as it is sometimes called, is predominantly used to join thin sheet metal components. The turned up edge lessens the heat distortion to the thin sheets. With the advent of cooler welding processes, the need for the edge joint has diminished.

The **saddle joint,** or **fishmouth joint,** is used to join structural tubing. The tubes may join at any angle, and more than two tubes may be part of the joint. A fillet weld is used, most often all the way around the joint.

Weld Symbols & Weld Types

Welding blueprints use specific symbols to denote weld types, locations, and other factors. The basic symbol consists of an arrow and a reference line with weld symbol. The weld symbol is placed above the reference line if the weld is located on the side opposite the arrow, and below the reference line for a weld located on the same side as the arrow. Weld symbols above and below the reference line indicate to weld both sides. A circle at the junction of the arrow line and reference line means to weld all around. Most hobby welders will not encounter these symbols.

The most common weld types used for home welding are the fillet and groove welds.

The **fillet weld** is roughly triangular in shape. It is made when welding most 90° angle joints. T-joints, open corner joints, lap joints, and saddle joints all take fillet welds.

The **groove weld** is made in a groove between pieces. The groove may be square grooved (straight sides), beveled (flat angled sides), or U shaped. The groove weld is used for butt joints, edge joints, and closed corner joints.

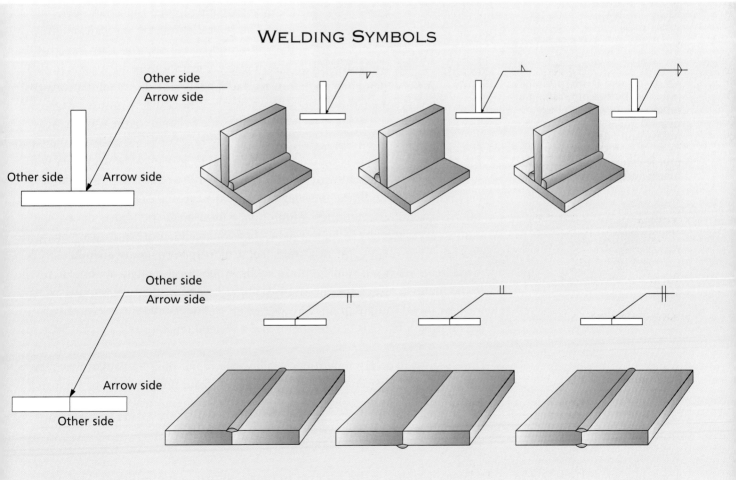

WELDING SYMBOLS

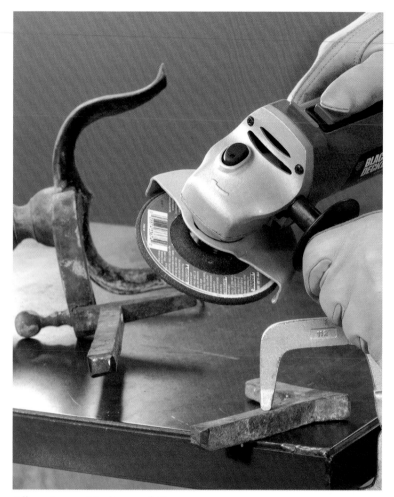

All parts need to be carefully prepared before attempting a repair. Paint needs to be ground or sanded off and grease and oil need to be cleaned away. This cast iron part is being beveled to allow greater weld penetration.

Repairing Metal

Once you begin welding, you will encounter numerous opportunities to repair items. When your friends and neighbors discover you can do repairs, even more challenges will come your way.

Performing welded repairs can be very tricky. It is important to assess your welding skills, the difficulty of the repair, and the intended use of the repaired item. Any structural or vehicle repairs, such as stairways, ladders, trailers, or truck chassis, need to meet the same safety standards as they did in their original condition.

The first step in considering a repair is determining why the item broke. If a weld was poorly executed, the repair might simply be to prepare the area and perform a good weld. If a piece has broken due to metal fatigue, simply "patching" over the crack will only cause more cracks outside the patched area. Cast iron and cast aluminum may have broken due to imperfections or inclusions in the casting, or they may have gone through rapid heating and cooling that caused cracking. Very often things break because they have been misused—which means your repair will likely be broken unless the behavior of the user changes.

The next step in a repair is determining what the base metal is. A magnet will be attracted to any metal with a certain concentration of iron in it, but stainless steel (which is sometimes non-magnetic), mild steel, and cast iron require very different welding techniques. Aluminum is non-magnetic and is discernable from stainless steel by its light weight—but which alloy is it? In the case of aluminum, some alloys are not weldable. Unfortunately, many manufactured metal items are made of alloys and may have been heat treated. Without access to the manufacturer's specifications, it might be impossible to determine what the base metal composition is. It is important to understand the effects of welding on these materials before attempting a welded repair.

Once you have determined the feasibility of a repair on a particular piece, the piece must be prepared carefully. All rust, paint, and finishes must be removed from the area of the weld, and, if you are arc welding, from an area for the work clamp. Grease and oil must be cleaned off. If the break is on a weld joint, the old weld bead needs to be ground down.

Mild steel is the easiest material to repair. Simply prepare the material as for any other weld, and weld using any of the welding processes.

Cast iron and cast aluminum need to be preheated before welding to prevent cracking due to temperature fluctuations. If the piece is small enough, you can put it in the oven and heat it to 400 to 500° F. Otherwise, use an oxyacetylene or propane rosebud tip. Temperature crayons, which melt at specific temperatures, are available for marking metal to be preheated. Cast iron can be brazed if the fit between the broken parts is good, or it can be braze welded or welded with shielded metal arc. Specific electrodes for cast iron are available. Cast aluminum can be brazed, braze welded, or welded with gas tungsten or gas metal arc welding. Allow cast parts to cool slowly after welding.

Some aluminum is not weldable. If the piece to be repaired has been welded, you can perform a welded repair. If you can determine the composition of aluminum parts, match the electrode or filler rod to that. Some filler rods and electrodes are multipurpose and can be used on more than one alloy. Gas tungsten arc welding is the best choice for aluminum, but it can also be welded with gas metal arc, or it can be brazed.

Stainless steel comes in numerous alloys, and it is important to match the filler material to the base metal. Do not clean stainless steel with a steel wire brush, as the mild steel wires may contaminate the stainless steel. Stainless steel is best repaired with gas tungsten arc welding, although it can be brazed as well.

If you are unsure of any aspect of a potential repair, consult with your welding supply dealer or an expert welder.

Remove the paint and finish from the weld area. If you are arc welding, also remove the paint from an area close to the weld for attaching the work clamp.

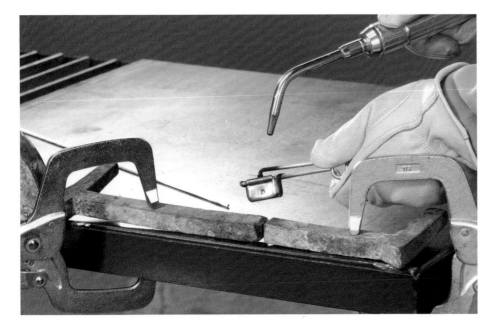

Cast iron can be braze welded as shown here, or shielded metal arc welded with cast iron electrodes. Either way, the metal needs to be preheated to 450° F before being welded.

WELDING & CUTTING PROCESSES

The following chapters give basic background information on the four major welding processes and two cutting processes that home hobbyists are most likely to use. Each chapter includes the equipment needed for the process and safety precautions. How-to photographs with step-by-step directions show specific techniques for each process. Tip sections offer suggestions for improving skills and keeping equipment in good condition. A separate chapter on electricity covers some basic points that are important to all of the arc processes.

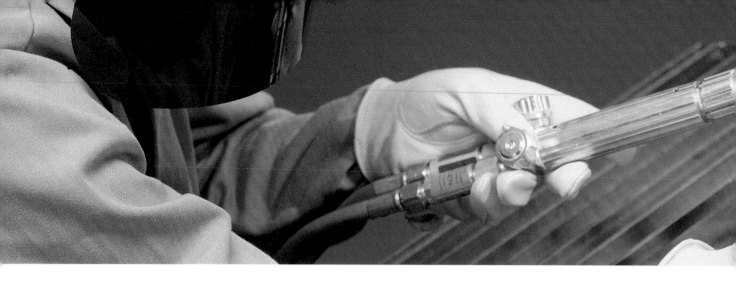

OXYACETYLENE WELDING

An oxyacetylene welding rig consists of two cylinders— oxygen and acetylene, regulators, hoses, and a torch with tip.

Oxyfuel welding is the process that uses the heat from a gas flame to melt base materials and cause them to join together. The gas flame is created by the combustion of oxygen and a fuel gas. Fuel gases are: acetylene, propane, butane, hydrogen, natural gas, and MPS (methyl acetylene-propadiene, formerly known as MAPP gas). Oxygen and acetylene burn in a neutral flame at a temperature between 5600° and 6300° F, the hottest of any gas flame and capable of melting most metals. Other oxygen-fuel gas combinations are hot enough to use for soldering and brazing, but not hot enough for welding. Oxyfuel welding with acetylene is called oxyacetylene welding, but it is often simply referred to as gas welding.

The oxyacetylene process is versatile, as it can be used for both welding and cutting materials (see page 68) as well as heating, soldering, and brazing. It can be much less expensive than arc welding and is very portable because it needs no electrical power source. Oxyacetylene can be used to weld any thickness of metal, but sections over ¼" are difficult to weld. Unfortunately, the techniques of oxyacetylene welding can be very hard to master, and there are serious safety concerns with the extreme flammability of acetylene and the high pressure gas cylinders.

Oxyacetylene welding equipment consists of an oxygen cylinder and an acetylene cylinder, each with regulators and gauges, oxygen hose, acetylene hose, torch, and tips.

Oxyacetylene welding may use fusion welding, where the base metals are melted together without filler material, or, more commonly, it may use a filler metal.

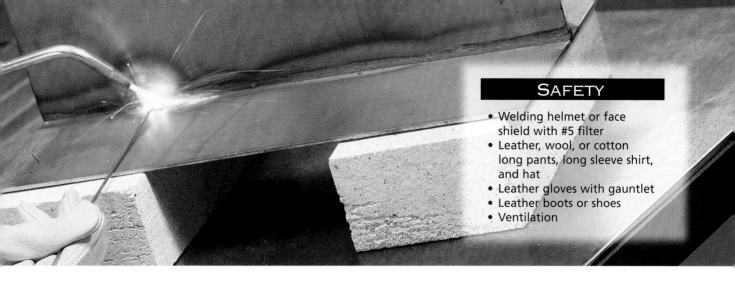

- Welding helmet or face shield with #5 filter
- Leather, wool, or cotton long pants, long sleeve shirt, and hat
- Leather gloves with gauntlet
- Leather boots or shoes
- Ventilation

THE EQUIPMENT

Cylinders. Oxygen comes in high pressure cylinders (sometimes called bottles or tanks) at 2200 pounds per square inch (psi) or more when full. The oxygen cylinder has a valve, and it always comes with a safety cap that screws on to the top to protect the valve. Never use the safety cap to lift an oxygen tank. The oxygen cylinder has a safety valve that will rupture to relieve tank pressure if the tank becomes overheated. Oxygen tanks should always be stored and transported in the upright position.

Acetylene. Acetylene is an extremely unstable gas. It cannot be pressurized above 15 psi in a free state. To safely pressurize the acetylene to 225 psi, the acetylene cylinder is filled with a porous material and acetone. When pressurized, the acetylene is absorbed by the acetone, which stabilizes it. When the pressure is released (the valve opened) the acetylene bubbles out of solution. Acetylene cylinders have fusible plugs that will melt in case of a fire and allow the gas to slowly escape rather than explode. Acetylene cylinders should always be stored in an upright position. Using an acetylene tank at an angle will allow acetone through the regulator and hoses, which will destroy them.

Cylinders should always be kept upright and secured with a chain or strap to prevent them from falling over. Never use a cylinder as a roller for moving heavy objects or for any purpose other than their intended use.

Cylinder Valves. Each type of cylinder has a valve that controls the flow of gas from the cylinder. A handwheel or valve wrench is used to open the valve. The oxygen cylinder valve should always be opened fully, as it is a backseating valve. A backseating valve is leakproof when closed and fully opened, but not otherwise. The acetylene valve should never be opened more than ¾ to 1½

Tools for oxyacetylene welding include fire bricks, pliers, striker, tip cleaner, and acetylene tank wrench.

turns. Less than this may lead to insufficient amounts of fuel and backflash; more than this makes it difficult to turn the acetylene off quickly in case of an emergency. If the acetylene valve is opened all the way, or opened suddenly, the acetone may escape from the cylinder, just like an overflowing soda can. Acetone can destroy the hoses and regulator fittings.

Pressure Regulators and Gauges. Pressure regulators reduce the pressure of the gas leaving the cylinder. A single-stage regulator reduces the cylinder pressure to working pressure in one step. A two-stage regulator reduces the cylinder pressure to working pressure in two steps. A two-stage regulator is better because it gives more precise control over gas flow. but it is substantially more expensive. The regulator adjusting screw turns clockwise to increase pressure and counterclockwise to reduce pressure. The regulator is completely off when the adjusting screw is loose or "backed out." Always back out adjusting screws as part of your post-welding routine.

Hoses. The flexible rubber hoses that move the gas from the regulator to the torch are designed to be leakproof and withstand high pressure. The oxygen hose is green, and the acetylene or fuel hose is red. Hoses are available either as a single hose or a dual hose where the oxygen and fuel hoses are paired together. The dual hoses are more common and more convenient. Always protect hoses from damage by moving them off the floor when not in use, keeping them behind the welding area so they are not burned with sparks, and keeping them out of traffic lanes so they are not stepped on or run over by vehicles. Hoses should not be allowed to come in contact with oily surfaces and should be protected from sunlight and chemical fumes to keep them in good condition. Always drain hoses when you have finished your welding session.

Oxygen and acetylene regulators (below left).

Available tips for an oxy-acetylene torch body include cutting head, rosebud heating tip, and welding tip (below right).

Fittings. Fittings connect the hoses to the regulator at one end and the torch at the other. For safety, the nut for the fuel hose (red hose) is left-hand threaded and has a groove machined around the nut. The oxygen (green) hose nut is right-hand threaded and has no groove. Never interchange the oxygen and fuel hoses or fittings. Never force a fitting—brass is a very soft metal, and it is easy to damage the fitting threads. Always hand thread and hand tighten fittings

before using a wrench, and be careful not to overtighten them. Never use pliers to tighten fittings, as they will damage the brass nuts.

Check Valves and Flashback Arrestors. Check valves and flashback arrestors are two safety features to prevent reverse gas flow or flashbacks. The check valve allows gas to flow from the hose to the torch. If gas pressure within the torch exceeds the hose pressure, a spring closes the valve to prevent back flow. In the event of a flashback, the check valve needs to be replaced. A flashback arrestor is installed between the torch and hose, and offers more protection than the check valve. The flashback arrestor prevents burning oxygen and fuel from flashing back into the hoses and regulator, which could cause an explosion. The flashback arrestor consists of a check valve, pressure-sensitive valve, stainless steel filter, and heat sensitive check valve. In the event of a flashback, the flashback arrestor does not need to be replaced.

Torch. The torch mixes and controls the flow of the fuel gas and oxygen. The torch consists of valves, torch body, mixing chamber, and tips. The torch is sometimes referred to as a blowpipe, but this is not technically correct.

Tips. Tips attach to the torch body and come in many sizes to create different size flames. A cutting tip, also called a cutting head or cutting torch, is attached to the torch body to use for flame cutting. A cutting tip has a number of holes for the preheating flames around a center hole for the pure oxygen. Cutting tips also come in a variety of sizes and with different numbers of preheating holes. Heating, or rosebud, tips are used to preheat metals to improve their weldability. Welding tips come in a wide range of sizes to match the thickness of the metal being welded. Matching the tip size to the welding material and gas pressure is critical for creating quality welds.

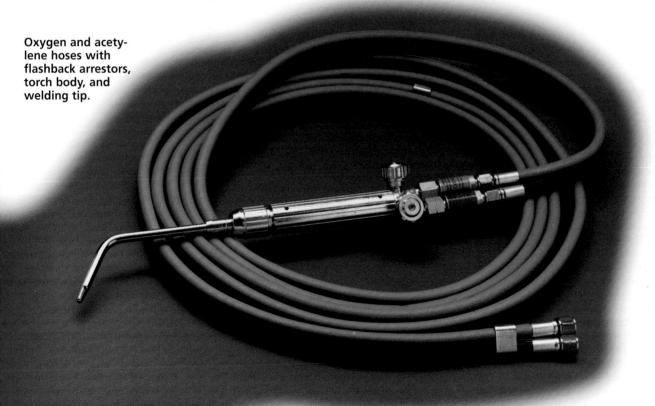

Oxygen and acetylene hoses with flashback arrestors, torch body, and welding tip.

Setting Up an Oxyacetylene Outfit

1 Secure the cylinders in an upright position, chained to a cart or strapped to a wall or post. Remove the protective cylinder caps. Wipe off the cylinder valve seats, regulator connections, and hose connections with a clean cloth. Crack open each cylinder valve briefly to expel any trapped dirt particles. "Flat top" acetylene cylinders (inset) may have antifreeze in the recessed valve seat. Use a clean rag to remove the liquid and dry the valve seat. This style acetylene cylinder requires a cylinder wrench to open the valve.

2 Attach the regulators to the cylinders. (The acety-lene connectors have left-hand threads.) Always hand tighten, then use a fixed wrench, not a pliers or an adjustable wrench, to tighten. Do not overtighten— a firm seating is all that is necessary. Attach the hoses to the regulators. The acetylene hose is red and left-hand threaded. The oxygen hose is green. NEVER use grease, oil, or pipe dope to lubricate fittings. Grease and oil can ignite spontaneously when they come in contact with oxygen—even without a spark or flame present.

3 Turn the regulator adjustment screws on the oxygen and acetylene regulators counterclock-wise until they are loose. (Some regulators may have a knob.)

4 Open the oxygen valve slowly all the way, while standing to the side in case the regulator gauge glass shatters. Turn the regulator adjustment screw until oxygen begins to flow through the hose, then loosen the regulator adjustment screw to stop the oxygen flow. Slowly turn the acetylene cylinder valve ¾ to 1½ turns.

5 Adjust the acetylene regulator valve until the gas begins to flow, then loosen the regulator adjustment screw to stop the flow. Attach the torch to the hoses. Be sure to pressurize the system and check for leaks before lighting.

Pressurizing (turning on) an Oxyacetylene System

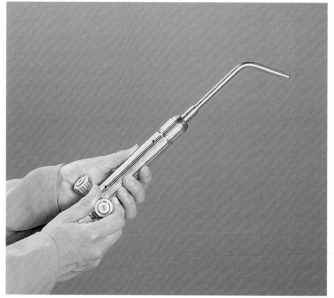

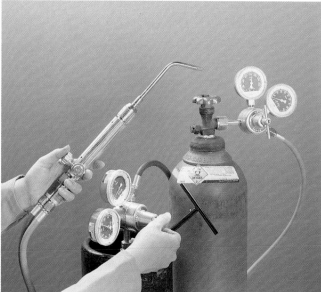

Make sure both torch valves are off. Turn both regulator adjustment screws counterclockwise until loose. Slowly turn the oxygen cylinder valve on. Once open, turn the valve all the way open to ensure proper seating without leaks. Turn the oxygen regulator adjustment screw clockwise until the gauge reads the desired pressure. (Refer to the manufacturer's specific instructions for operating pressures.) Open the oxygen valve on the torch to check the flowing oxygen pressure. Adjust if necessary and close the torch valve. Slowly open the acetylene cylinder valve ¾ to 1½ turns. (Leave the wrench on the valve if it is a wrench-style valve.) Turn the acetylene regulator pressure adjustment screw until the desired pressure reads on the regulator gauge. Open the acetylene valve on the torch briefly to make sure the flowing pressure matches the desired working pressure. If not, adjust the regulator until the proper pressure is reached.

Checking for Leaks

Apply leak-detecting solution to all connections with a small brush. (You can use soap and water so long as the soap is not petroleum based.) If any connections cause bubbles in the solution, tighten the connections and check again.

BACKFIRE & FLASHBACK:

Backfire and flashback are two hazardous situations that can be caused by improper gas pressures. Backfire is the pre-ignition of the acetylene and oxygen inside the tip that causes a popping sound. This may damage the tip or spray molten metal from the weld area. Flashback is the flame burning backward into the torch or hoses, causing a popping or squealing noise. Flashback can cause an explosion in the hoses. Avoid both hazards by matching the tip size to the material being welded and by using the proper pressure settings. Using lower pressures than recommended can cause backfire and possibly flashback.

Pre-lighting Checklist:

- Make sure torch valves are closed.
- Turn both regulator adjustment screws counterclockwise until loose.
- Slowly turn on the oxygen cylinder valve all the way. Turn the regulator adjustment to the proper pressure.
- Slowly turn the acetylene cylinder valve 1½ turns. Turn the regulator adjustment valve to the proper pressure.

Some welders have been taught to open both the acetylene and oxygen valves before lighting the torch to avoid the smoky acetylene flame. This practice is no longer recommended.

NEVER light a torch with a match or butane lighter.

Lighting the Torch

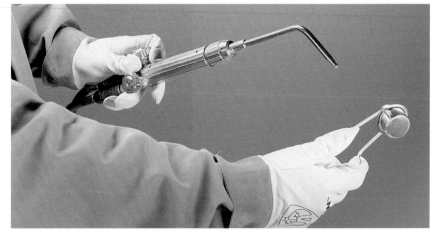

1 Hold the torch in one hand with the thumb and forefinger on the acetylene torch valve. Hold the striker in front of the torch about 3" to 6" away at a slight angle. Turn on the acetylene torch valve ¼ to ½ turn.

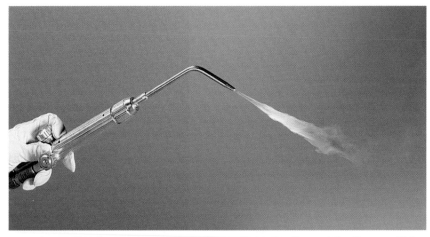

2 Immediately use the spark lighter to light the flame. The flame will be yellow and smoky.

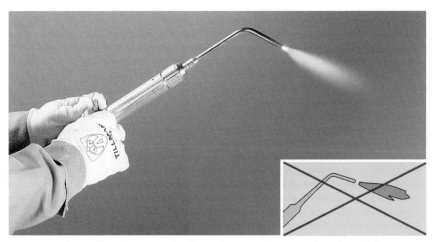

3 Put the striker down and adjust the acetylene torch valve with your right hand so the flame is burning without producing soot. The flame should not be separated from the torch (inset). Open the oxygen torch valve slowly. Adjust the oxygen to get a bright white inner flame and a bluish outer flame. Turn down the acetylene to eliminate the excess acetylene feather if present. When you have finished welding, turn off the oxygen first, then the acetylene.

Flame & Flame States

The flame of an oxyacetylene torch has two parts—the inner or primary flame and the outer or secondary flame. The flame has different temperatures at different locations. The outside edges are cooler because they are burning with the ambient air, which is only 21% oxygen. The torch tip is cooler because complete combustion hasn't been reached. The hottest area is the tip of the primary or inner flame cone. Here the gases are completely combusted and are insulated by the secondary flame. There are three flame states for the oxyacetylene flame: carburizing, neutral, and oxidizing.

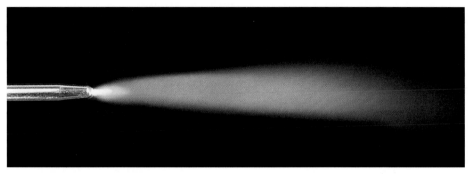

The carburizing or reducing flame has an excess of fuel. This is a useful flame as it will break down metal oxides to get at the oxygen, thus cleaning the weld area to a small degree. This process adds carbon to welds, which makes them harder. The carburizing flame has a bright white primary flame, an acetylene "feather" around the primary flame, and a bluish white secondary flame with orange edging.

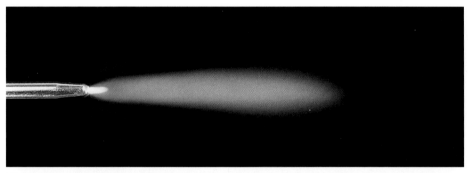

The neutral flame is the exact point where the feather and the inner cone come together. In this flame, there is exactly enough oxygen present to provide total combustion of the fuel gas. Most welding and cutting operations use a neutral flame. The neutral flame has a bright white primary flame and a colorless to bluish secondary flame.

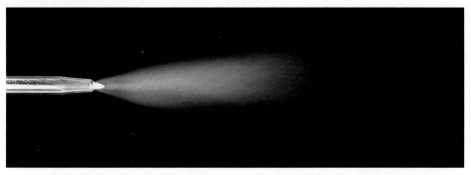

The oxidizing flame has an excess of oxygen. The white cone of this flame is small and pointed and somewhat paler than the neutral flame. A hissing sound often accompanies this flame. This flame is not particularly useful as it hastens oxidizing, which is not desirable in welding. It can, however, be used for removing carbon from molten metal, thus softening the metal.

Pre-welding Checklist:

- Check hoses for damage before pressurizing the system.
- Prepare metal for welding by wire brushing or sanding off mill scale and rust. Use acetone or denatured alcohol to remove oil or other chemical residues.
- Use fire bricks to avoid unnecessary heat loss and prevent welding to the welding table.
- See manufacturer's recommendations for appropriate tip sizes and gas pressures.
- Set up materials and clamp if necessary.

NOTE: The directions for oxyacetylene welding are for right-handed welding. Reverse the directions for left-handed welding, or if you find it easier to manipulate the filler rod with your right hand.

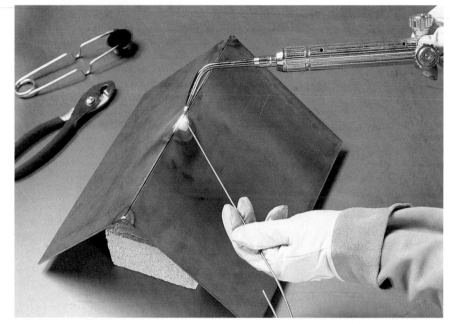

1 Select an appropriate filler rod and lay it on the table next to the bricks. Light the torch and adjust to a neutral flame. Pull down your face shield. Place small fusion tack welds at each end of the joint and in the middle if it is a long joint. (A fusion weld uses no filler rod.) Turn off the torch, oxygen first then acetylene, and check that your tacked piece is still in the desired position. If not, use a hammer to move it into position or break the tack weld and reposition.

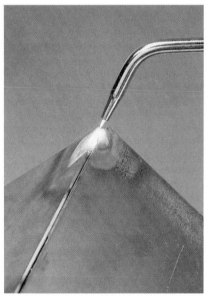

2 With the torch at a 45° angle to the right and oscillating the torch in a ¼" to ½" circle over both metal pieces, create a weld puddle at the right end of your workpiece.

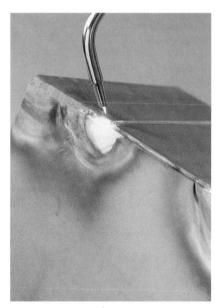

3 When a molten puddle has formed, move the filler rod close to the puddle and flame, but not in it. Begin moving slowly to the left while oscillating and maintaining the molten puddle. Dip the filler rod into the middle of the molten puddle and remove it, but keep it within the heat zone.

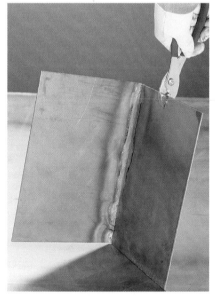

4 Continue dipping, oscillating, and moving to the left. As you reach the end of the weld, the cumulative heat build-up may make it necessary to adjust to a shallower angle to deflect heat away from the puddle and prevent burn through. When finished, turn off the oxygen torch valve first, then the acetylene torch valve. The weld should penetrate to the back without burning through.

Depressurizing an Oxyacetylene Outfit:

When you have finished welding, or if you are going to stop welding for more than 10 or 15 minutes, depressurize your setup. The hoses and regulators are designed to leak small amounts of fuel and oxygen if they are pressurized and not being used, so it is important for safety and economy to depressurize them. You will soon be so comfortable with the pressurizing and depressurizing steps that it won't seem like an inconvenience at all. It is important to do the fuel gas and oxygen in separate steps, to prevent having mixed, unburned oxyacetylene in the torch.

- Close the fuel gas cylinder valve.
- Open the fuel gas torch valve until both gauges read zero.
- Loosen (counterclockwise) the fuel gas regulator adjustment screw.
- Close the fuel gas torch valve.
- Close the oxygen cylinder valve.
- Open the oxygen torch valve until both gauges read zero.
- Loosen (counterclockwise) the oxygen regulator adjustment screw.
- Close the oxygen torch valve.

Oxyfuel Tips

GAS OPTIONS:

The most useful fuel gas for oxyfuel welding is acetylene. Its neutral flame generates the highest heat and heat concentration with the lowest chemical interactions with the molten metal. Other fuel gases, such as MPS or MAPP and propylene can be used for brazing and cutting applications. Natural gas and propane can be used for brazing and heating operations. Make sure that the equipment—hoses, regulators, torches, and tips—are designed for use with the gas you choose.

GAS	DENSITY (Air = 1)	TEMPERATURE OF NEUTRAL FLAME WITH OXYGEN
Acetylene	0.906	5589° F
Methylacetylene-propadiene (MPS)	1.48	5300° F
Natural gas	0.62	4600° F
Propane	1.52	4579° F
Propylene	1.48	5250° F

FIRE BRICKS:

Fire bricks are specially made bricks that have little water content so they will not explode when heated to high temperatures. Fire bricks do not pull the heat from your weld or braze, and you cannot weld your material to them.

Maintenance. The primary maintenance for oxyacetylene welding equipment is cleaning the torch tip. A dirty tip will spark, pop, and often direct the flame sideways. Tip cleaners are inexpensive sets of cleaning rods used to clean the various sized tip orifices (see photo, page 27). The set usually comes with a small file to smooth the tip. To clean, simply insert the correctly sized tip cleaning rod into the orifice, and pull back and forth. Do not rotate the tip cleaner as this may enlarge the orifice. Also, do not use drill bits to clean tips. The sharp edges of the bit will cut grooves into the tip. Cleaning rods have smoothed edges and are sized especially for tips. Do not clean tips while the torch is lit.

Brazing

Brazing is very similar to soldering since flux is applied to tightly fitted metal parts that are then heated to the point where filler material will melt and be drawn into the joint. Silver soldering and hard soldering are terms incorrectly used to refer to brazing. Brazing is different from soldering because it takes place at temperatures over 840° F and below the melting point of the base metals. The metals are not fused, but held together by the filler metal adhering to the base metals through capillary action.

There are a number of industrial brazing processes, such as dip brazing, furnace brazing, and induction brazing. The home welder is likely only to do torch brazing. Torch brazing can be done with an oxyfuel torch using acetylene as the fuel gas, or any of the other fuel gases (see page 35). NOTE: Different fuel gases require different regulators, hoses, torches, and tips.

For brazing to work, the gap between the parts must be between 0.002 and 0.010 inches. If the gap is too tight, the flux and filler will not flow evenly through the joint. If the gap is too big, the strength of the joint is lessened. Gaps between parts can be measured with a feeler tool, available at automotive stores. Items to be brazed must be absolutely clean and free from rust, corrosion, grease, oil, and cleaning compound residues.

Brazing is often used commercially to join dissimilar metals such as tungsten carbide saw teeth to a steel saw blade. Another common use for brazing is in lugged bicycle frames. Because nearly every metal can be joined using brazing, it is highly suitable for art applications.

Brazing supplies include flux and silver solder (left). Braze welding requires flux coated rods, or separate flux and rods.

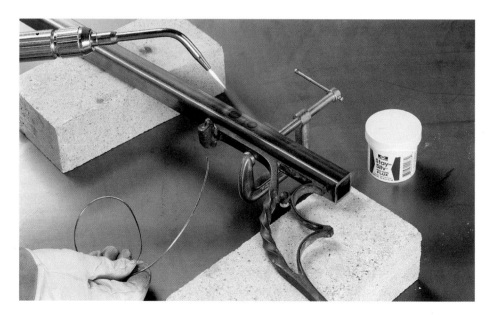

Thoroughly clean and flux both sides of the joint area. Using a small torch tip, heat the entire joint area until the flux turns clear and starts to run. Add enough filler metal to fill the joint. (Silver alloy is shown.) After the metal has cooled, the flux residue can be removed with hot water.

Braze Welding

Braze welding is similar to standard oxyacetylene gas welding except the parent or base metals are not melted, so there is no molten puddle. Instead of a steel alloy filler rod, a flux coated brass filler rod is used. Braze welding is often incorrectly referred to as brazing. Braze welding does not use capillary action to pull filler material into the joint—the filler metal is deposited as fillet or groove welds.

The brazing rod is melted by the heat of the metal and the flame, but it should not be held in the flame itself. The parts for braze welding should fit tightly, but the gap is not as important as with brazing.

Braze welding is used for joining dissimilar metals and for metals of different thicknesses. This technique is often used to repair cracked or broken cast iron.

Braze welding has less distortion than oxyacetylene welding because less heat is applied to the parts. A disadvantage is that it is not as strong as welding where the base metal is melted, but a well-made braze weld is still sufficient for most non-structural applications. Because the base metals do not need to be melted, braze welding can be done with any of the fuel gases listed on page 35.

If you are creating a piece that will be welded and braze welded, you must be careful to complete the non-brazed welds first. The heat involved with all other welding processes will boil off the brass alloy of a braze weld, ruining the weld and creating toxic fumes.

1 Braze welding is useful for joining thin metals, like this expanded metal, to thicker metals. Heat both parts, directing more heat toward the thicker part. It may take a long time for the thicker metal to heat. Using fire bricks will prevent a metal table top from absorbing any heat.

2 When both parts glow a dull cherry red, touch the flux coated rod to the joint. The flux and the filler metal will melt. If the metal is molten or the fluxed rod comes in contact with the flame, the flux will burn and the filler metal will boil. This results in a poor joint in addition to giving off toxic fumes.

ELECTRICITY FOR WELDING

Arc welding and cutting processes—shielded metal arc, gas metal arc, gas tungsten arc welding, and plasma cutting—all use electricity to generate the necessary heat. Understanding electricity is not necessary to use these processes, but knowing basic terms and concepts will help you understand why certain welding events occur.

Electric current is the flow of electrons through a conductor from a high concentration of electrons (negative charge) to a low concentration of electrons (positive charge). As electricity flows through a conductor, it generates heat based on how much resistance the conductor offers. An arc is simply a sustained electrical discharge across an air gap. Because air is highly resistant to electron flow, an enormous amount of heat is generated by the movement of electrons across this gap. The heat generated by an arc is in the area of 11,000° F, but about half of this heat is dissipated.

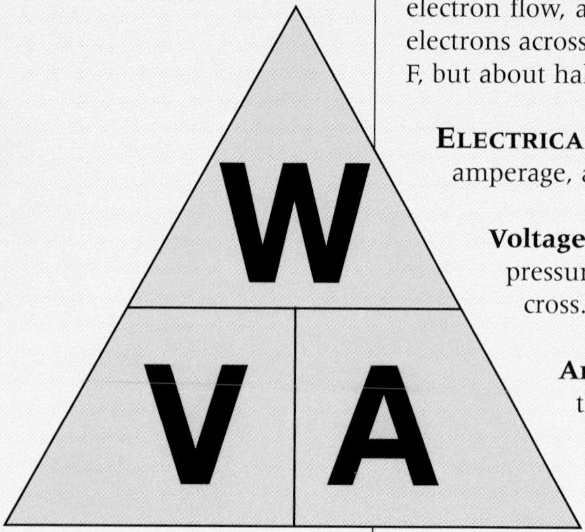

ELECTRICAL UNITS. The units used to refer to electricity are voltage, amperage, and wattage.

Voltage or volts (v) is the measure of electric potential or the electric pressure. The voltage controls the size of the air gap that the arc can cross. The higher the voltage, the larger the gap the arc can cross.

Amperage or amps (a) is the volume of electrons flowing through a conductor. The amperage controls the size of the arc.

Wattage or watts (w) is the measurement of the amount of electrical energy or power contained in the arc. Wattage affects the width and depth of a weld.

WELDING POWER. Power for welding may be supplied in one of the following ways:

Constant Voltage (CV). The arc voltage is maintained even when the current (amps) changes. This means if the arc length is changed, which changes the current flow, the voltage stays relatively the same.

Constant Current (CC). As the amperage fluctuates, the voltage increases or decreases to keep the total power (wattage) output the same.

OPEN CIRCUIT AND OPERATING VOLTAGE. The open circuit voltage is the voltage that exists at the electrode tip when the machine is on but no arc has been struck. The higher the open circuit voltage, the easier it is to strike an arc. Open circuit voltage is usually between 50 and 80 volts. The higher the voltage, the greater the risk of electrical shock.

Volts, amps, and watts are related to each other in such a way that volts × amps = watts.

The operating voltage is the voltage when the arc is struck and the circuit is completed. This is usually between 17 and 32 volts depending on the arc length, the type of electrode, the type of current, and the polarity.

POWER SOURCES FOR WELDING. There are three sources for producing the low-voltage high-amperage combination that arc welding needs.

A mechanical generator produces power through the use of a gasoline or diesel engine.

A step-down transformer takes available high voltage alternating current and changes it to a low-voltage high-amperage current.

An inverter uses solid state electronics to change the current without the weight of a transformer.

CURRENTS USED FOR WELDING. The type of current used and the polarity is important to welding.

Alternating Current (AC) is standard available household current. The electron flow changes direction two times per cycle. Welding with AC means that the electrode and the workpiece alternate between positive and negative, so the welding heat is distributed evenly to both. This balances penetration and build-up.

Direct Current (DC) electrons flow in one direction only. A rectifier is used to convert alternating current to direct current. With direct current, there are two polarity options:

Direct Current Electrode Negative (DCEN)—formerly called straight polarity—means the electrode is negative, the workpiece is positive; electrons are flowing from the electrode to the workpiece and the heat is concentrated in the electrode.

Direct Current Electrode Positive (DCEP)—formerly called reverse polarity—means the electrode is positive, the workpiece is negative; the electrons are flowing from the workpiece to the electrode. DCEP produces the best welding arc characteristics.

DUTY CYCLE. The duty cycle is the amount of continuous running time at a given power output for a welding machine, given as a percentage for a ten minute period. Because welding machines produce heat internally, they need a certain amount of cooling time. A 60% duty cycle means that a machine can run continously at that setting for six minutes, then it will need to cool for four minutes. Duty cycle is critical in construction and industrial applications, and it can be important for home shop use. A 10% duty cycle at the maximum setting means one minute of welding and nine minutes of cooling. This could be a problem for large projects on thick material. The higher the duty cycle, the more expensive the machine.

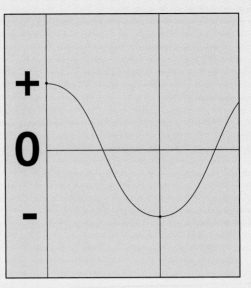

Alternating current alternates between positive and negative polarities, passing through a zero, or no current point, between the two.

NOTE:

Work leads and work clamps are sometimes referred to as ground leads and ground clamps. This is not technically correct, as the electricity is not being grounded. Instead, the work lead and clamp are allowing for completion of the circuit back to the machine.

SHIELDED METAL ARC WELDING

Shielded metal arc welding (SMAW) is also referred to as arc or stick welding. The process involves the heating of the base metal to fusion or welding temperature by an electric arc that is created between a covered metal electrode and the base metal. The coating or covering on the electrode provides both flux and shielding gas for the weld. The electrodes come in 9" to 15" straight lengths in a range of wire thicknesses from $\frac{1}{16}$" to $\frac{3}{8}$", hence the name "stick." SMAW is used extensively for fabrication, construction, and repair work because the machinery is inexpensive and fairly simple, and the electrodes are inexpensive. There are drawbacks to SMAW: It doesn't work well on thin materials (less than $\frac{1}{8}$" is difficult), electrodes need to be changed frequently as they are used up, and the protective slag coating must be chipped off each weld.

Safety. Shielded metal arc welding uses electricity, so there is always the possibility of receiving an electric shock or being electrocuted. When an electrode (stick) is placed into the electrode holder, it is "live." If the electrode touches anything that the work clamp is in contact with, the circuit will be completed and an arc will be struck. To prevent this from happening, always remove the electrode from the holder when you are not actively welding. Do not use your bare hands to insert or remove electrodes—always touch electrodes with dry gloves. Remember that water and electricity never mix well, so do not weld while standing on a wet or damp floor or ground, and do not weld outdoors in the rain. The electrode will be hot after use, so take care where you dispose of electrode stubs. A metal bucket is a good addition to your SMAW workshop.

A shielded metal arc welder consists of a power source, electrode holder, and work clamp.

- Welding helmet with #10 to #14 filter
- Leather, wool, or cotton long pants; leather jacket
- Heavy-duty welding gloves
- Safety glasses
- Hat
- Leather boots or shoes
- Ventilation

SMAW welding produces ultraviolet and infrared rays, harmful fumes, and hot spatter. Protect your eyes with a #10 to #14 filter in a full-face welding helmet or hood. Heavy-duty leather welding gloves and a welding jacket with leather sleeves are necessary to protect you from the molten spatter. Proper ventilation from an exhaust hood or fan is important since many of the chemicals used in the electrode coatings are hazardous if inhaled. Also, it is a good idea to screen off your welding area so others are protected from the intense light of the arc.

The Equipment. SMAW machines are available as either alternating current (AC), direct current (DC), or with the capability of switching between the two. The machine itself is simple in that it merely converts high-voltage low-amperage line current into low-voltage high-amperage welding current. Output is controlled with one knob. You often will hear SMAW machines referred to as "buzz boxes."

AC welding machines meet most home and small shop needs, are inexpensive, and are readily available. Because the alternating current cycles through a zero current between the positive and negative polarities, it can be difficult to strike and maintain an arc. DC machines are easier to use and have many home and hobby applications, but they are more expensive. Because DC current can have its flow reversed (see page 39), a DC machine has more versatility in terms of the electrodes that can be used. This allows for a wider range of welding positions, metal thicknesses, and metal types that can be welded. This versatility makes a DC shielded metal arc welder well worth the extra expense.

Useful tools for shielded metal arc welding are a pliers, chipping hammer, and wire brush.

The equipment itself consists of the welding machine, which usually has one adjustment knob, an electrode lead with electrode holder (sometimes called a stinger), and a work lead with work clamp. You will often see work leads and work clamps referred to as ground leads and ground clamps. The work lead and clamp are not grounding the electricity, they are completing the circuit back to the machine.

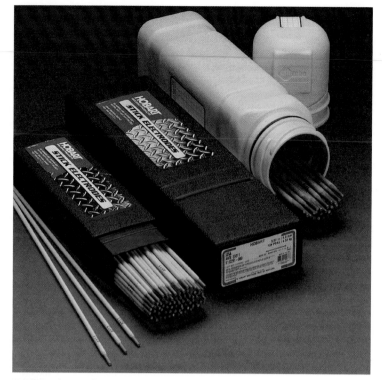

SMAW electrodes are sold in 5- or 10-pound boxes. Specialty electrodes may be bought a pound at a time. It is important to keep electrodes dry, either in the original box or a storage container.

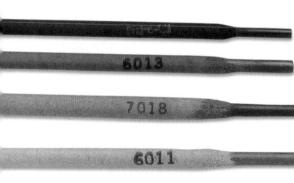

Electrodes for SMAW are stamped with a numeric code.

SMAW Electrodes. SMAW electrodes are solid, round, metal wires coated with flux and other components. In addition to producing shielding gas and flux, the covering may also contain additional metals for filler or alloying elements for the weld.

The American Welding Society (AWS) publishes standards for the electrodes. Electrodes come in diameters ranging from ⅟₁₆" to ⅜" in increments of ⅟₃₂". The electrode diameter measures the wire itself, not the diameter of the wire with the covering. The electrode designation is inked onto the covering near the bare end of the electrode. The number classification for SMAW electrodes begins with the letter E because they are electrodes. The first two or three numbers on the left denote the tensile strength of the properly completed weld in thousands of pounds per square inch. The second number from the right indicates the welding position appropriate for that electrode: 1 = all, 2 = flat grooves and flat or horizontal fillet weld, 3 = flat only, 4 = all. The last two numbers designate the current and polarity uses and other special notes. There also may be electrode suffixes that denote alloys that have been added to the electrode.

Each electrode manufacturer may have a number of electrodes of a specific AWS designation that are slightly different and have been tailored to specific uses. The diameter of the electrode will determine which amperage to use. Use the manufacturer's guidelines to determine amperage. If not available, start with 90 to 120 amps minimum range for a ⅛" electrode and add 40 amps for each ⅟₃₂" increase in diameter. This will give you a rough minimum starting amperage.

The most commonly used electrodes are 6011, 6013, 7014, and 7018. The 6011 and 6013 electrodes will work with AC power, the 7000 electrodes will not. For a beginner, 6013 with DC power is generally the easiest electrode to use in terms of striking an arc and maintaining a consistent arc. It is always a good idea to talk with your welding supplies dealer about what type of welder you are using, the type of welds you are making, and the materials you are working on to get the best electrode for your purposes.

Slag. Shielded metal arc welding produces a weld that is covered with a coating of ceramic-like slag. The flux and other components in the covering clean the material to be welded and also float out impurities in the weld. These impurities and flux solidify on top of the weld which protects the cooling weld from the effects of oxygen in the atmosphere. The slag must be scraped or chipped away before the weld bead is covered with another weld layer or before the weld is painted or finished. Safety glasses should be worn during this procedure.

Shielded Metal Arc Welding

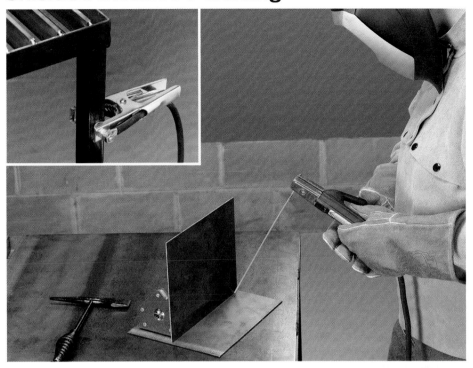

1 Set up your material to be welded. Make sure the electrode holder is not touching the workpiece or worktable. Attach the work cable clamp to the table (inset) or workpiece. Turn on machine. Adjust the range switch for the desired amperage. Wearing leather gloves, place an electrode in the electrode holder. Position the electrode over the area to be tacked, flip down your helmet, and tap or scratch the electrode on the area to be tacked to strike an arc. After making your tack welds, remove the electrode from the electrode holder. Check to see that the tacked pieces are aligned properly. If not, use a hammer to move them into alignment or break the tack welds and retack. Chip slag from tack welds so it does not contaminate the final weld.

2 Replace the electrode in the electrode holder, and position the electrode over the left side of the area to be welded. Hold the electrode at a 10° to 20° angle to the right. Flip down your hood and scratch or tap to strike an arc. The distance between the metal and electrode should not exceed the thickness of the electrode bare wire diameter. Move slowly to the right until the weld is completed.

3 To remove slag, hold the workpiece with pliers at an angle and scrape or knock the slag with the flat blade of the chipping hammer. Wear safety glasses when chipping slag.

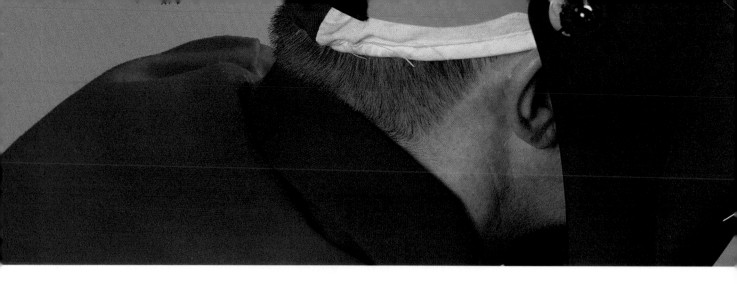

GAS METAL ARC WELDING

Gas metal arc welding (GMAW), also referred to as MIG (metal inert gas) or wire feed, is a process where a consumable electrode (wire) is automatically fed through a welding gun along with a continuous flow of a shielding gas. The actual application of filler metal is achieved with most small machines through the short circuit transfer method. Other transfer methods used by more powerful machines are short circuit globular and spray pulse.

The GMAW process has a number of advantages. The gun or torch can be held at a uniform distance from the weld, unlike shielded metal arc welding where the distance from the electrode holder to the weld becomes shorter as the electrode is consumed. The trigger power control on the welding gun also makes it possible to be completely positioned and ready to weld without accidentally striking an arc. When ready to weld, the welder can flip down the helmet and pull the trigger without getting off target. Because the electrode is the filler, the welder does not need to coordinate a filler rod in one hand and the torch in the other. The GMAW gun can be held steady with both hands to create a uniform bead. Because of the shielding gas, GMAW welds are smooth and clean, with no slag to chip or grind. The GMAW process can operate at very low amperages and is a relatively cool welding process, so 22 and 24 gauge sheet metals can be welded without distortion. The process also requires narrower beveling for thicker plate welds, so less time is spent on grinding.

A gas metal arc welding setup consists of a power source, wire feed, work cable with clamp, supply cable with gun, and gas cylinder with regulator.

Some disadvantages of GMAW are that the shielding gas nozzle does not allow for welding in tight spaces without some modifications. Because the shielding gas can be disrupted or blown away by drafts easily, the process is not suited for working outdoors.

THE EQUIPMENT

Power supply. In the small GMAW units, the power supply and wire feed are integrated into the same cabinet. In larger, multipurpose machines, the wire feed is a separate unit. The power supply converts the standard alternating current (AC) into direct current (DC). Alternating current is not appropriate for gas metal arc welding because its constantly switching flow does not yield a steady, consistent arc. On the machine, you will be able to adjust the voltage, polarity, and wire feed rate; the machine adjusts the amperage. When using the power source to weld with a shielding gas, the machine should generally be set up for electrode positive, that is, the electrode is positive and the workpiece is negative. If used without shielding gas and with flux cored wire, the polarity usually needs to be switched to electrode negative. This is achieved by switching the contact wires within the machine. Larger, multipurpose machines may have a switch to change the polarity. Always check manufacturer's recommendations for polarity settings.

Wire feed. The wire feed consists of a spool of wire, a tension controller, and rollers and a roller motor. The wire speed is set by the speed adjustment knob, depending on the thickness of the material being welded. The rollers have V or U grooves sized to match particular wires. Most machines come with two-sided rollers that can be switched over to handle two different size wires.

Gun. The GMAW gun, sometimes referred to as a torch, is attached to the welding machine via the supply cable. The cable carries the power, the power control, the wire in a special liner, and the shielding gas. The gun has a trigger that turns the power on and off, which also starts the wire feed and the shielding gas flow. The gun generally has a goose neck shape, although straight neck and

A MIG pliers is a handy tool for gas metal arc welding.

The wire feeding mechanism consists of a spindle to hold the wire spool, drive wheels, rollers, and a tension adjustment. Most welders now have a reference chart with recommended settings.

A spool gun is used for feeding aluminum wire because it often breaks or misfeeds through a standard cable. A standard gas metal arc gun consists of a handle, gas diffuser, contact tip, and nozzle.

flexible neck guns are available. A contact tip is screwed or cam locked into the gun. This tip has an orifice the same size as the wire being used. It is important that this be sized correctly—too large and good electrical contact between the source and the electrode will not be made, too small and the wire will not fit. The shielding gas is directed toward the work area with a nozzle. On most home versions, the relationship between the contact tip and the gas nozzle stickout is not adjustable; larger welders have a wider variety of nozzle sizes and shapes. It may be worthwhile to purchase an aftermarket adjustable system. When using the GMAW process, it is important that the supply cable be kept as straight as possible to prevent kinking the wire or impeding the gas flow.

The final piece of equipment is the work cable with clamp. This is clamped to the workpiece or to a metal work surface that the piece sits on to complete the circuit.

Electrodes. When choosing an electrode (wire), consider the composition properties, cleanliness of the base metal, and the shielding gas. If you will be welding out of position, this will also be a factor. There are dozens of wire choices for GMAW.

Most home GMAW welders use 1-pound or 10-pound wire spools. Larger spools are generally less expensive.

Electrodes are labeled with alpha-numeric codes that describe their type, tensile strength of the weld, whether it is solid or tubular (tubular is flux cored), and chemical composition. For mild steel, ER70S-3 is a good general purpose wire. ER70S-4 and ER70S-6 are good wires for dirty or rusty metals. Wire also is available for welding aluminum and stainless steel. Available wire sizes are 0.024, 0.030, 0.035, and 0.045 inches.

Using a wire feed machine without shielding gas requires the use of flux cored wire (often called innershield), and the process is then called flux cored arc welding (FCAW). Because the wire makes the electrical contact as it travels through the contact tip, the flux must be inside the wire, which makes flux cored wire more expensive than regular GMAW wire. Commercial welders may use a "dual shield" flux cored wire that does use a shielding gas. Welds made with this process are as clean as regular GMAW welds.

Flux cored arc welding can be done outdoors because there is no shielding gas to be disturbed by wind and weather. Unfortunately, using flux cored wire results in a less attractive weld due to the presence of slag and more spatter. The flux cored wire usually has greater penetration and is often used to stretch the capabilities of a small welding machine. Because 0.035" is the smallest diameter for flux cored wire, it is not appropriate for welding thin sheet metal. The lowest setting for this size wire is still too hot for this application.

Shielding Gas. The shielding gas for GMAW is supplied by a cylinder with a flow regulator and connecting hoses. The gas line is connected to the welding machine, which directs it through the cable.

Carbon dioxide is suitable for general GMAW welding. It gives good penetration and is inexpensive compared to other gases. Argon and carbon dioxide in a 75% argon and 25% carbon dioxide mix is the standard GMAW shielding gas. It is slightly more expensive than pure carbon dioxide, but it yields welds with less spatter. Pure argon is used for shielding aluminum welds. If you choose to use pure carbon dioxide, select an electrode that performs well with this shielding gas.

Gas Cylinder Safety. Gas cylinders store compressed gases at pressures up to and greater than 2000 psi. This is sufficient pressure to send a tank through a concrete wall if the cylinder valve should be damaged. It is important to be extremely careful with gas cylinders even when they hold the non-flammable gases used in GMAW welding. Gas cylinders should always be upright and chained or strapped to a wall, post, or cart. Never drag a cylinder; never lay one down or roll it flat. To move a cylinder, chain it to a handcart first. If you must move a cylinder without a handcart, tip it slightly and roll it. Never weld anything to the cylinder or safety cap—and be careful to never accidentally strike an arc against a cylinder. If you do, you will have to purchase that cylinder.

A flow meter registers gas flow with a small floating ball.

Setting Up the Wire Feed

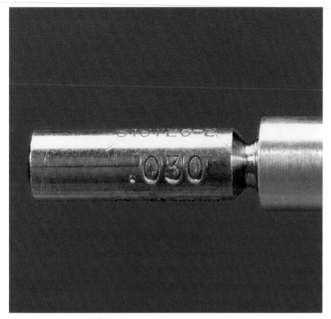

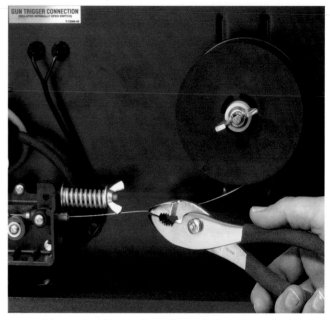

1 Contact tubes are stamped with their size. Make sure the contact tube and the drive roll grooves are the correct size for the electrode you are using. Place the wire spool on the spindle, and secure it with the pin lock, lock ring, or wing nut. Make sure it is feeding in the proper direction.

2 After releasing and cutting off the crimped wire end, hold the wire firmly with a pliers. The wire is tensioned and the entire spool will rapidly unroll if you do not hold it firmly. Swing the tension arm or pressure roll out of the way. Push the wire through the inlet wire guide, through the groove on the drive roll, and out through the outlet wire guide.

NOTE:
Unless your machine has an inch switch for advancing wire or a purge switch for activating gas flow, you will use the gun trigger to accomplish both tasks. Using the gun trigger means the wire is "live" and will arc to anything the work clamp is touching.

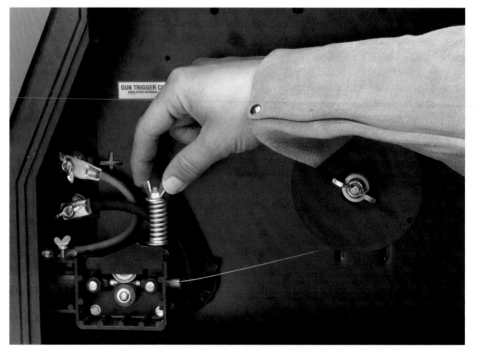

3 Swing the tension arm or pressure roll back into position. Adjust tension according to manufacturer's directions. On a new machine, the drive roll pressure will already be set. Make sure the wire is aligned perfectly straight—not up and down or side to side—on the drive roll. Turn the machine on, turn the wire speed to its highest setting, pull the cable straight, and depress the trigger. Some machines have an inch button that feeds the wire without supplying power to the contact tip or wasting shielding gas while loading wire.

Setting Up the Shielding Gas Flow Meter

1 Open the cylinder valve briefly to clear out any dirt. Wipe the cylinder threads with a clean, dry cloth.

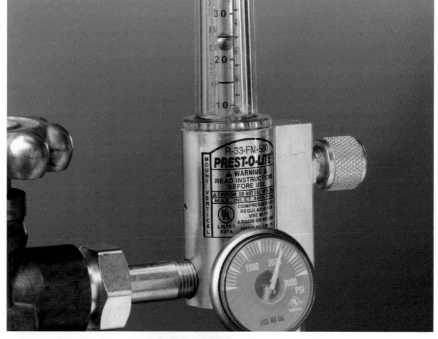

2 Attach the flow meter to the cylinder. Use a fixed wrench to prevent damaging the brass fittings.

3 Turn the knob on the flow meter clockwise to tighten it so no gas can flow through it. If the flow meter is open when you open the cylinder valve, the high pressure can damage the flow meter.

4 Attach the hose to the flow meter and to the welding machine. Slowly open the cylinder valve, then, once it is open, open the cylinder valve completely. To set the flow rate, turn on the machine. Depress the trigger to activate the gas flow, and turn the flow meter knob counterclockwise. While gas is flowing, continue turning the knob until the meter registers the proper flow rate. Make sure that the flow meter or flow gauge is rated for use with the shielding gas you are using. For example, an argon/carbon dioxide flow meter cannot handle pure carbon dioxide.

- Gun, shielding gas, and machine cables, hoses, and connectors are tight.
- Polarity is set correctly for type of wire being used.
- Cables are in good condition.
- Supply cable is straight and unkinked.
- Gas regulator and flow meter are correctly installed.
- Contact tube is in good condition.
- Spatter has been cleaned from nozzle and contact tube (see page 40).

Gas Metal Arc Welding

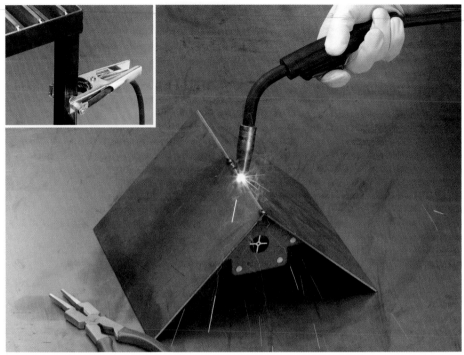

1 Prepare and fit up the material to be welded. Attach the work cable clamp to your welding table (inset) or the workpiece. Turn on the machine and shielding gas. Adjust the wire speed and voltage according to the manufacturer's recommendations. Cut the electrode to ⅜" stickout. Put the tip of the electrode at the point of the first tack weld, flip down your helmet, and pull the trigger. Place tack welds evenly around the weld area. Trim the electrode for proper stickout at the end of each use. Check to see that the workpiece is still aligned properly. If not, adjust with a hammer or break the tack welds and retack.

2 Start at the left end of the weld. Hold the gun with both hands and position it at a 20° angle with the tip pointing to the left. Put the tip of the electrode at the beginning of the weld, flip down your helmet, and pull the trigger.

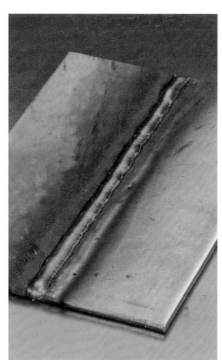

When you have finished welding with a GMAW rig, it is important to shut it down properly so you are set for your next welding session. If you do not turn off your shielding gas, you will lose much of it to bleed off even if you weld the next day.

- Close the gas cylinder valve.
- Press the gun trigger or purge switch until the flow meter or flow gauge reads zero.
- Turn off the flow meter.
- Turn off the machine.
- Coil the supply and work cables and store them off the floor.

3 Begin welding, moving steadily to the right. GMAW has a distinctive sizzling sound. Popping and snapping indicate dirty material or an improper voltage or wire speed adjustment.

4 A finished GMAW is smooth with even ripples or weave pattern, no slag, and little spatter.

FLUX CORED ARC WELDING:

Flux cored arc welding uses the same wire feed and power supply as gas metal arc welding but usually without the gas shielding. This is convenient for welding outdoors in windy conditions, but the weld is not as clean. To use flux cored wires, most welding machines need to be converted. Usually this involves changing the output polarity, and installing a gasless nozzle. It also might require installing proper drive rolls and a different cable liner. Otherwise, follow the same steps to weld with flux cored wire as with solid wire.

Flux cored wire welds are covered with a layer of slag.

Maintenance & Troubleshooting

A small amount of maintenance on your GMAW equipment will result in better, more consistent welds and longer lasting equipment. Spatter—tiny pieces of the electrode or base metal that have sizzled off—builds up on the nozzle and the contact tip. Remove this spatter frequently as you weld so it does not interfere with gas flow or electrical conductivity. Turn off the machine, remove the nozzle, and use the closed point of the MIG pliers (page 45) to ream out the nozzle and file the end of the contact tip. An anti-spatter gel is available in which to dip the hot nozzle and contact tip. Anti-spatter spray can be used to coat the contact tip and the nozzle. This spray is also useful for coating your welding table to prevent spatter from sticking to your work surface. Eventually you will need to replace the nozzle, but regular maintenance and proper welding techniques will extend the life of a nozzle considerably.

Contact tubes become worn because they are a soft copper alloy and the electrode is steel. The electrode will wear through the contact tip, possibly making the electrical flow irregular. Contact tips should be visually inspected for wear on a regular basis. The orifice on a worn contact tip will appear oval instead of round. Tips generally are good for about eight hours of continuous welding use. NOTE: Always turn off the welder before changing the contact tip.

Use dippable anti-spatter gel to prevent spatter build up on the nozzle and contact tip. Simply dip the hot nozzle into the gel.

It is important to keep the welder fan motor and rectifier free of dirt and dust to prevent it from overheating. If your welder is stored in a dusty shop, or you use it infrequently, keep it covered. Use low pressure air to blow dust and dirt from these assemblies. Use a vacuum to remove dirt from the wire feed mechanism.

The supply cable needs to be cleaned occasionally as well. Check the manufacturer's recommendations for frequency, but they generally recommend cleaning after you've used 50 pounds of flux cored wire or 300 pounds of solid wire. With the power off, remove the cable from the machine. Remove the gas nozzle and contact tip from the gun, lay out the cable straight, and use low pressure air to blow into the gun end. (Using high pressure air may create a dirt plug that will clog the cable permanently.)

Always store the supply and work cables and the gas hose off the floor and away from chemicals, hot sparks, and sunlight.

REMOVING A BIRD'S NEST:

A "bird's nest" is a tangle of wire in the wire drive mechanism. This happens when the wire drive rolls continue feeding wire but the cable is blocked, the outfeed tube is misaligned, the wire is stubbing out on the base metal, or the wire has been welded to the contact tip. The drive rolls are set to slip in these cases, but if the tension has been adjusted too tightly, they may continue to push wire.

To fix a bird's nest, turn off the machine and cut the wire as it comes off the spool. Remember the wire is under tension, so you must hold the spool end, then tie it off through one of the spool holes. The tangled wire also may be storing tension, so it may fly out of the drive roll area. Release the tension arm or roller arm. Pull the wire out of the drive mechanism and the supply cable. Wear safety glasses when removing a bird's nest.

A "bird's nest" is a tangle of wire in the drive roll mechanism.

STUB OUT OR STUBBING:

"Stub out" is when the electrode welds to the base metal without melting or breaking off. This is caused by the voltage being too low, the wire feed being set too fast, or holding the gun too close to the work when starting. Correct the settings, grind off the stub outs, and restart the weld.

Stub out results in short sections of wire poking out of the weld.

GMAW TROUBLESHOOTING:

PROBLEM	SOLUTION
Wire feeds, but no arc can be struck	• Check to see that work clamp is connected
Weld bead is full of holes like a sponge (porosity)	• Make sure shielding gas is on • Adjust shielding gas to a higher flow rate • Eliminate drafts • Verify correct polarity
Weld bead is tall and looks like a rope	• Make sure voltage setting is appropriate for the material's thickness • Reduce your travel speed
Excessive spatter or dirty welds	• Reduce the gun angle • Hold the nozzle closer to the work • Decrease voltage
Arc starts and stops	• Check the wire feed for steady feeding • Check cable connections • Clean the weld materials

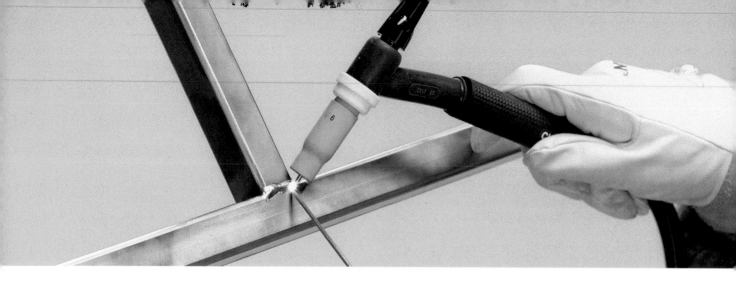

GAS TUNGSTEN ARC WELDING

Gas tungsten arc welding (GTAW), commonly called TIG (tungsten inert gas), and sometimes referred to as Heliarc (the L-TECH trade name), is a process that generates an arc between a non-consumable tungsten electrode and the workpiece. The electrode and the weld are protected by a shielding gas, and filler metal may or may not be used.

Gas tungsten arc welding differs from the other arc welding processes because the electrode is non-consumable and not used as filler material. GTAW is more like oxyfuel welding in terms of the skills needed to manipulate the torch with one hand and the filler rod with the other. GTAW requires another layer of coordination because most machines also use a foot activated amperage control.

Like gas metal arc welding, gas tungsten arc welding is a clean process because the shielding gas eliminates the need for flux and the resultant slag.

Safety. Because gas tungsten arc welding is such a clean process, welders often are tempted to weld without gloves or in short sleeve shirts. This is not recommended. The arc most likely produces more ultraviolet rays than other processes, and because there are no fumes or smoke, those rays are entirely unfiltered. It is important to cover all exposed skin to prevent UV burns. Filter requirements are a minimum #10 shade, and if you have an auto-darkening hood, be sure that it is rated for the GTAW process. Some entry level auto-darkening hoods are not. The arc may produce ozone, which is hazardous to breathe over long periods. Make sure your gloves, clothes, and work area are dry. Always turn off the power when changing electrodes.

A gas tungsten arc welding setup consists of a power source, work cable and clamp, supply cable and torch, foot control, and gas cylinder with regulator.

The Equipment. The basic equipment needed for GTAW is a constant current welding machine, cable with torch, work cable and clamp, electrode, and inert gas cylinder with regulator and flow meter. Optional equipment includes a remote amperage control and a water cooled torch with water cooler and hoses.

Although a mid-range shielded metal arc machine can be used to deliver the current for gas tungsten arc welding, a dedicated, good quality GTAW machine delivers the current as AC or DC, provides an optional high frequency output for no touch arc starting, has a remote control option for foot pedal control, and has a solenoid for shielding gas control. The combination of AC and high frequency makes it possible to weld aluminum with good results. The newest electronic GTAW machines have advanced current control capabilities and are becoming more and more affordable.

Torch & Cables. The GTAW torch holds the electrode and delivers the shielding gas. It can be air or water cooled. The torch parts are the cup or nozzle, collet body, collet, end cap, and torch body. The collet and collet body hold the electrode firmly and establish electrical contact with the electrode. The cup directs the shielding gas. A torch may be air cooled for use below 200 amps, but over 200 amps the torch usually is water cooled. The supply cable supplies electricity, shielding gas, and coolant to the torch. This may be an integrated cable or individual cables. A work cable with clamp is also necessary.

Some GTAW torches have flexible necks, which allows them to be bent into the most convenient angle for supporting the torch. Unfortunately, the non-flexible torches will bend if forced, and then they will be ruined. Some torches also have a gas on/off valve. This is necessary for machines that are simply power sources with no internal gas flow controls.

The collet body, collet, end cap, and cups all come in a variety of sizes. The collet body and collet are sized to match electrode diameters. Each part is stamped with its size. The end caps come in a

Pliers and a stainless steel wire brush are handy for gas tungsten arc welding.

variety of lengths—some accommodate an entire 7" electrode, others are shorter for more clearance while welding.

Cups come in a variety of sizes denoted by $\frac{1}{16}$" increments. A #4 nozzle is $\frac{4}{16}$", a #8 is $\frac{8}{16}$". Cups should ideally be 4 to 6 times the size of the electrode. A cup that is too large will not direct the gas in a proper stream, a cup that is too small may not provide adequate steady flow. A gas lens or screen in the torch balances the gas flow. Good shielding designs allow you to use a lower gas flow. Higher flow creates turbulence and jetting, which disturbs the shielding—more does not equal better when it comes to shielding gas flow. Cups also are available in different lengths. A

A gas tungsten arc welding torch includes the electrode, collet body, collet, cup, backcap, and torch body with heat shield.

longer nozzle increases the electrode extension from the collet, which may increase the electrode temperature. Use either lower amperage or larger diameter electrodes if you are using a longer nozzle. Shorter nozzles may be necessary for tight working conditions. Nozzles are also available in clear (fused quartz) types, which are more expensive but give greater visibility, especially in cramped quarters.

Shielding Gases. Two inert shielding gases are used for gas tungsten arc welding: argon and helium. They may be used alone or in combination with one another. Argon yields better starts and better arc maintenance. Helium gives a hotter arc and allows faster travel speeds. Helium, however, is very expensive. Argon and helium are both contained in standard cylinders, and a pressure regulator flow meter combination will need to be attached. Because of the density difference between the two, either a separate flow meter needs to be used for each, or use a flow meter that has calibrations for each type of gas. Argon flow rates for up to $\frac{1}{8}$" steel is 8-10 cubic feet per hour (CFH), for stainless steel 11-13 CFH, and 12-20 CFH for aluminum. Drafty locations may require higher flow rates. Check the manufacturer's recommendations.

Electrodes. The electrode for gas tungsten arc welding is always a tungsten or tungsten alloy rod with either a pointed or rounded end. The electrodes come in a variety of diameters.

Preparing the Electrode. Prior to use, the cut end of the electrode must be sharpened to a point or melted to a ball. The tip may be ground to a point or chemically sharpened. The electrodes come in 7" lengths. To increase the number of points available,

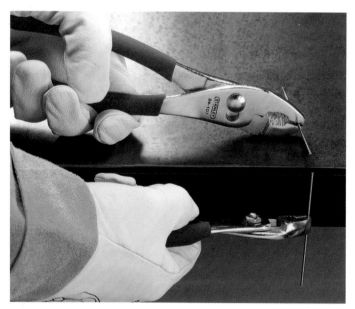

Tungsten is very brittle, so electrodes can be scored with a file, then snapped over a sharp table edge.

ELECTRODE CHARACTERISTICS:

ALLOY	AC/DC	TRAITS & USES	COLOR
Pure tungsten	AC	• Welding of aluminum • Forms ball at tip	Green
1% Thorium oxide (thoriated)	Primarily DC, but also AC	• Easier arc starts • Carries more current • Low level radioactive	Yellow
2% Thorium oxide	DC	• Long life • Easier arc starts	Red
Zirconium oxide	AC	• Similar to pure tungsten but carries more current	Brown
2% Cerium oxide (ceriated)	DC	• Not as good as thoriated but not radioactive	Orange
Lanthanum oxide	DC	• Similar to ceriated	Black

score the electrode with a file or cut-off wheel, and snap it in half. Tungsten is very hard but brittle, so it is easy to grasp each end of the electrode with pliers and snap it in half over a sharp table edge.

Because all tungsten electrodes look and feel the same regardless of their composition, it is important to keep them clearly separated by type. The color codes will wear off, or, if you point each end of your electrode, be ground off. It is helpful to have clearly labeled containers for each type of electrode.

Two critical factors in grinding the electrodes are the grinding wheel and the grinding direction. You must use a hard, fine grinding wheel dedicated exclusively to tungsten.

Metal particles left on the wheel from grinding aluminum or steel would contaminate the tungsten, which causes erratic arc behavior and poor weld quality. An extremely hard material, tungsten will become hot as it is ground. Sharpen the electrode tip so that grinding marks run lengthwise down the tip, not in a circular or crosswise pattern. Lengthwise grinding focuses the electron flow toward the tip; circular grinding causes the arc to be unfocused and possibly jump sidewise from the electrode rather than off the tip point. Chemical means also can be used to sharpen tungsten by dipping a hot tungsten rod into a chemical agent. The length of the taper on the tungsten tip should be two to three times the diameter of the tungsten.

To safely hold tungstens for sharpening with a grinder, insert them into the chuck of a drill. Running the drill while sharpening the tungsten ensures a uniform point. Move the tungsten across the wheel to prevent grooves in the wheel face.

Chemical sharpeners are available for sharpening tungsten.

Welding with AC current requires that the tip of the electrode be balled, which is accomplished by running DC electrode positive or AC current and striking an arc on copper or brass. The ball should not extend beyond the diameter of the electrode, although many sources recommend a ball one and one half times the diameter of the tungsten.

If you touch the weld puddle or filler rod with the electrode during welding, you must change to a fresh electrode. Any time the electrode tip becomes pitted or blackened, is no longer pointed, or the ball becomes too large, you must change to a fresh electrode. This will happen often, so it is best to have a number of electrodes sharpened and ready to go. If you forget to turn on the shielding gas or the flow is interrupted, the electrode will give off a thick yellow tungsten oxide smoke. This smoke is hazardous, so resume welding only after the smoke has cleared. You will need to change electrodes if this happens.

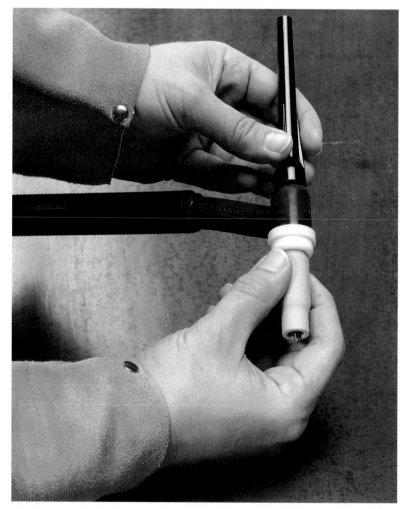

Tightening the back cap locks the tungsten electrode into place. The tip of the electrode should extend beyond the end of the cup by a distance of three times the electrode's diameter.

Anatomy of the GTAW Machine

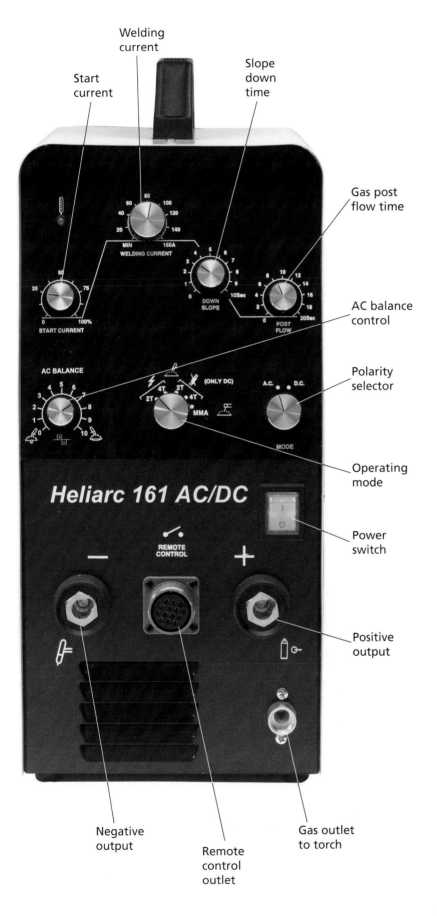

Welding current

Start current

Slope down time

Gas post flow time

AC balance control

Polarity selector

Operating mode

Power switch

Positive output

Gas outlet to torch

Remote control outlet

Negative output

Heliarc 161 AC/DC

Setting Up the GTAW Machine:

Dedicated GTAW machines, like this one and the one pictured on page 54, have many advanced features. The basic setup, however, is the same.

The positive and negative output receptacles are for the torch and work clamp connections.

The gas outlet connects to the torch gas hose.

The remote control socket is for the foot or finger control. Using a remote control allows the welder to control the amount of current while welding.

The operating mode selects high frequency or scratch starts.

Polarity selects either AC or DC.

AC balance control allows for adjusting AC power to be more positive or more negative to create either more cleaning action or deeper penetration. Advanced machines can adjust the AC power to be as much as 90% positive or negative, rather than the 50% for standard AC power.

Start current controls the current for arc starting.

Welding current sets the range for welding. The foot or finger control then operates within this range.

Slope down time gradually reduces power to the arc without extinguishing the arc. This allows for the weld crater to fill before the arc is extinguished.

Gas post flow controls how long the shielding gas will flow after the arc is extinguished.

Pre-welding Checklist:

- If using a water cooled torch, check for leaking.
- Check all cables for wear and damage.
- Clean and fit up parts to be welded.

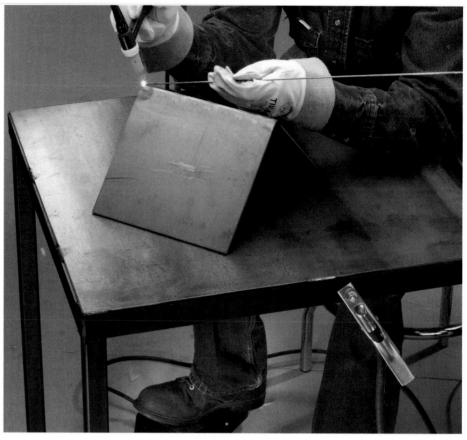

1 Set the controls based on manufacturer's recommendations for the material to be welded. Turn on the machine, and turn on the water pump, if available. Attach the work clamp to the welding table or workpiece. Flip down your helmet, activate the foot or finger control if using one, and strike an arc by scratching the tip of the tungsten against the base metal. If your welder has a high frequency option, you do not need to scratch start the arc. Place a tack weld at each end of the joint to be welded. You may be able to tack the joint by simply fusing the two pieces with the heat of the torch, or you may have to use filler rod.

STRIKING AN ARC:

Unless you have a high frequency option, you will need to physically strike an arc—called a scratch start. Rest the cup on the workpiece at a sharp angle. Move the tip until it briefly contacts the work, then angle it back again to start the arc. After the arc is started, lift the cup off the workpiece and establish the proper torch angle.

High frequency allows the arc to jump the gap without needing to create physical contact between the electrode and the workpiece.

2 Position yourself to weld from right to left (if you are right handed) with the torch at a 15° angle to the right of center. Hold the filler rod in your left hand. Position yourself so you can comfortably hold the torch and filler rod for the duration of the weld.

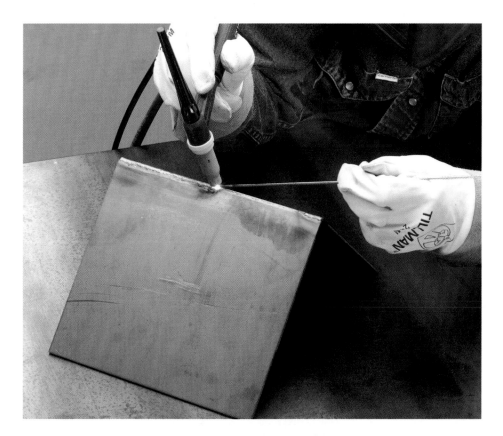

3 When a molten puddle has formed, dip the tip of the filler rod into the middle of the molten puddle. Keep the filler rod at a low angle to prevent disturbing the shielding gas. Keep the tip of the filler rod near—but not in—the puddle. Move the electrode to the left and continue the melting and dipping process.

Post-welding Sequence:

- Turn off cylinder valve.
- Purge gas from gas line.
- Turn off flow meter or gauge.
- Turn off machine.
- Coil hoses and cables off the floor.

4 As you approach the end of your weld, you may need to adjust your travel speed because the buildup of heat in the material makes the molten puddle form more quickly at the end of the weld than at the beginning. You also may need to adjust the torch angle to be more shallow (not shown here) so that less heat is directed into the base metal.

Troubleshooting

Filler metal for gas tungsten arc welding comes in rod form and ranges from ¹⁄₁₆" to ³⁄₁₆" in size. Rods are available in a variety of alloys, including aluminum, chromium and chromium nickel, copper, nickel and nickel alloys, magnesium, titanium, and zirconium. Specific alloy compositions are available for creating specific weld types on specific base metals. These filler metals are similar to those used in oxyfuel welding, with the exception of the carbon steel rods, which are not copper coated as they are for oxyfuel.

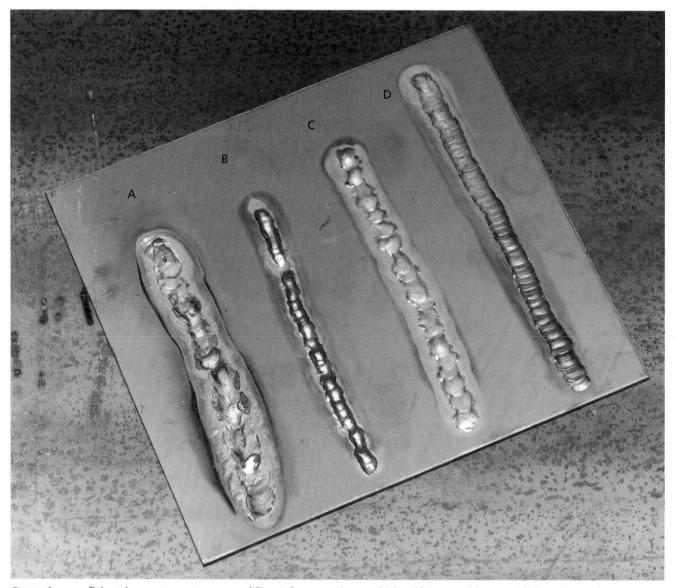

Becoming proficient in gas tungsten arc welding takes practice, and identifying problem welds is an important step. Weld A is too hot. Increase the travel speed or decrease the amperage. Weld B is too cold and is simply sitting on top of the base metal rather than penetrating it. Decrease the travel speed or increase the amperage. Weld C was done too quickly. Travel speed needs to be controlled and consistent. Weld D is a good quality weld with even ripples, good penetration, and a moderate crown.

A well-done gas tungsten arc weld on aluminum has even ripples and good penetration. This sample weld shows two passes to create a fillet weld on ¼" stock.

GTAW TROUBLESHOOTING:

PROBLEM	SOLUTIONS
Weld looks porous or sooty	• Make sure shielding gas is on and is correct type • Make sure shielding gas cylinder is not empty • Eliminate drafts • Make sure base metal is totally dry • Clean base metal thoroughly • Increase gas flow rate
Base metal distorts	• Tack weld parts before welding • Clamp parts down to rigid surface • Scatter welds to diminish heat buildup
Unstable arc	• Adjust electrode to work angle • Clean base metal thoroughly • Clean electrode • Connect work clamp to workpiece • Bring arc closer to work
Electrode is rapidly consumed	• Make sure polarity and current settings are correct • Increase electrode size • Increase gas flow • Decrease current • Increase gas post flow time • Use proper shielding gas

PLASMA CUTTING

Plasma cutting and welding are arc processes. Plasma is a gas that can conduct electricity because it is in a highly ionized form. The gas transfers the arc, but because of the constriction of the gas, the gas resistance is very high, which creates the extreme heat for plasma processes. Plasma cutting uses a very constricted arc to melt the base metal while compressed air or other gas blows the melted metal out of the kerf. This process can be used on any conductive metal—aluminum, brass, cast iron, copper, steel, stainless steel, and titanium—which sets it apart from oxyacetylene cutting, which is only useable on oxidizable metals.

Though the plasma arc temperature is 40,000° F, it is so constricted and the cutting speed is so fast that the thermal distortion to the metal being cut is low. Plasma cuts are clean and are often weldable with no additional clean up if the base metal was initially clean. Properly done, the kerf is fairly straight sided, and no slag is present.

Safety. Plasma cutting produces sparks, smoke, and fumes. When cutting materials that contain chromium and nickel (such as stainless steel) or materials that have been galvanized or zinc coated, many toxins will be present in the fumes. When cutting through painted, bonded, or dirty metals, these surface additions often burn off, producing hazardous smoke. Plasma cutting often produces ozone and various nitrogen oxides that are colorless and can be odorless; both are hazardous. Therefore, good ventilation is important even when plasma cutting.

A plasma cutter consists of a power source with a compressed air or inert gas connection, work cable with clamp, supply cable, and torch.

SAFETY

- Welding helmet with #8 filter
- Leather, wool, or cotton long pants, long sleeve shirt, and hat
- Heavy duty welding gloves
- Leather boots or shoes
- Ventilation

Plasma cutting may not seem as bright as other arc processes, but it is. It produces ultraviolet rays, so it is important to protect your skin and eyes. Because of the high level of open circuit voltage, plasma cutting has added electrical shock hazard. Make sure all surfaces around the cutting area are dry and all your clothing and gloves are dry. Turn off the power to the machine before changing any torch parts.

Never cut containers, tanks, or cylinders that may have held flammable materials. Even a small amount of flammable residue can cause an enclosed vessel to explode when cut.

Equipment. Plasma cutting machines are expensive, but as technological advances are made and demand increases, more companies are introducing smaller, less expensive home and small shop equipment. If you regularly need to cut stainless steel, aluminum, or the high strength steel now used in automobile bodies, this machine can be worth the cost. Small, 115-volt plasma cutters are available that will cut up to ⅜" material. Larger, 220-volt machines can cut thicker materials and have higher duty cycles. Aluminum and stainless steel require higher amperages, so check whether the machine easily can cut the materials with which you typically work.

A dehumidifying filter is very important for the compressed air source for plasma cutting.

Most plasma cutters require a compressed air source. Any shop air compressor that can deliver 65 psi is sufficient. It is critical that a filter be installed to keep the air dry and oil free. Follow the manufacturer's directions for installing the filter. Some plasma cutters have an internal air compressor. These units often require more maintenance than models that utilize a separate compressor.

The plasma torch consists of a shield cup, cutting tip, starter cartridge, electrode, and torch handle. Most plasma torches have a manual switch on the torch body. The cutting tip and electrode are consumable parts. Check them frequently for wear and replace them when necessary.

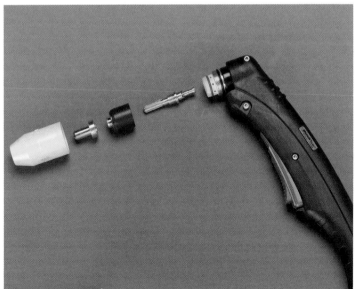

The plasma cutting torch consists of (left to right) a shield cup, cutting tip, starter cartridge, electrode, and torch handle.

Pre-cutting Checklist:

- Compressed air fittings are tightly attached.
- Cables are in good condition.
- Ventilation is sufficient to remove fumes from cutting area.
- Work area is dry.
- Flammable materials are removed from area.
- Sparks and slag from cutting will be contained.

1 Check the manufacturer's recommended settings for the material to be cut. Arrange the material on a cutting table and determine the most comfortable cutting position. Attach the work clamp to the workpiece or welding table. Dry run through the cutting motion to practice speed and cutting position.

2 Check manufacturer's directions for arc starting procedure. Most current machines are designed to drag the nozzle directly on the material's surface. Activate the arc and hold the torch perpendicular to the surface of the material. Move steadily and smoothly along the entire length of the cut. Do not stop the arc until you have passed through the end of the cut.

3 A good plasma cut has squared edges, small vertical ripples, and little or no slag.

Troubleshooting and Techniques

A high-quality circle cutting attachment for a plasma cutter is expensive, but worth the investment if you will be making repeated circle cuts. This unit comes with a magnetic pivot holder for steel and a suction cup pivot holder for all other metals.

TIP:
Making a good-quality plasma cut is dependent on a consistent travel speed. Consult the owner's manual for cutting speeds for different material thicknesses and amperage settings. With the machine off, practice moving across the planned cut at the correct speed.

PLASMA TROUBLESHOOTING:

PROBLEM	SOLUTIONS
Arc does not start	• Connect work clamp to workpiece • Turn on power source • Tighten cable connections • Make sure electrode is in working condition
Cut does not penetrate through material	• Cut more slowly • Make sure torch is held perpendicular to material • Make sure machine is capable of cutting that thickness • Increase amperage setting • Verify correct air flow and pressure
Excessive slag or dross	• Increase cutting speed • Decrease torch standoff distance • Replace worn torch parts • Adjust amperage setting
Torch parts consumed quickly	• Install or replace air filter to prevent oil or water from reaching torch • Cut metal within the capability of the machine • Make sure gas pressure is correct

OXYACETYLENE CUTTING

Oxyacetylene cutting uses acetylene and oxygen to preheat metal to a temperature of 1600° F, then uses pure oxygen to burn away the heated metal. Because the cutting is achieved by oxidation of the metal, oxyacetylene cutting only works on metals that are readily oxidized at this temperature. Metals that can be cut with the oxyacetylene process are mild steel and low alloy steels. Oxyacetylene cutting can be used to cut thicknesses from less than ⅛" up to 12". Oxyacetylene cutting is inexpensive compared to machine cutting. It is very portable because no external power source is necessary, and it is faster than machine cutting. It is, however, limited to steel. The molten slag presents a fire and burn hazard, and the heat input to the base metal may cause distortion or changes to the properties of the steel.

Safety. The risk of starting a fire or being burned is high with oxyacetylene cutting. It is important to prevent molten slag and sparks from coming into contact with skin and flammable materials. Make sure you are wearing heavy-duty leather gloves with gauntlets, a leather jacket or leather-sleeved jacket, and leather boots. The work area should be cleared of flammable materials. If an item will be cut in place, make sure surrounding areas are protected from heat, sparks, and dropping slag. Never cut sealed tanks, cylinders, or items that have contained flammable materials. Never cut near gasoline tanks or fuel lines.

The Equipment. The basic equipment for oxyacetylene cutting is the same as for oxyacetylene gas welding, with the addition of a cutting torch or cutting attachment. An oxyacetylene cutting setup consists of an oxygen cylinder, an acetylene cylinder, regulators and hoses, and a torch with cutting attachment or a dedicated cutting torch. Cutting attachments and dedicated cutting torches have levers to activate the oxygen flow.

Oxyacetylene cutting equipment consists of two cylinders—oxygen and acetylene—regulators, hoses, and a cutting torch with tip.

SAFETY

- Full-face #5 filter
- Leather, wool, or cotton long pants, leather jacket, and hat
- Heavy-duty welding gloves
- Leather boots or shoes
- Ventilation

Cutting Torch & Tips. Most oxyacetylene welding sets come with a cutting accessory that attaches to the torch body in the same way that the welding tips do. A dedicated cutting torch is a one-piece unit that has its own mixing chamber. Its greater overall length allows for more distance between the heat zone and the operator, and it can handle higher oxygen flow rates. A dedicated cutting torch is usually fairly expensive and not necessary unless very thick metals will be cut, which requires greater oxygen flow.

Both the cutting torch and the cutting attachment take a variety of cutting tip sizes. The cutting tip has a number of preheat holes surrounding the pure oxygen orifice. It is important to match the cutting tip to the thickness of the metal being cut. A welder often takes a one-size-fits-all approach to cutting tips, which always results in poor-quality cuts. Thinner metals require fewer preheat holes and a smaller oxygen orifice; thicker metals require more preheat holes

A striker, tank wrench, pliers, and tip cleaner are needed for oxyacetylene cutting.

and a larger oxygen orifice. Cutting tips are made of copper and can be damaged easily. They need to be cleaned regularly with an appropriately sized tip cleaner.

Fuel Gas Options. Because the metal being cut does not need to be brought to the melting point, various gases other than acetylene can be used. Propane, natural gas, propylene, and methylacetylene-propadiene can be used as the preheating fuel source. Each of these gases requires specific regulators and may require different torches and torch tips. Check manufacturer's recommended usage before substituting an alternate fuel gas.

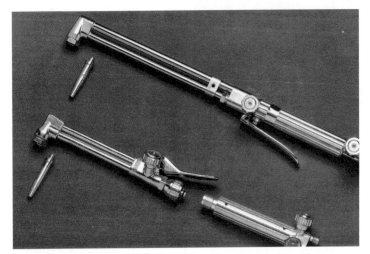

A dedicated cutting torch (top) is a one-piece unit with one oxygen and one fuel-gas valve. A cutting tip is attached to a standard torch body (bottom) and includes an additional oxygen valve. A range of tip sizes is available for both torch styles.

How to Cut with Oxyacetylene

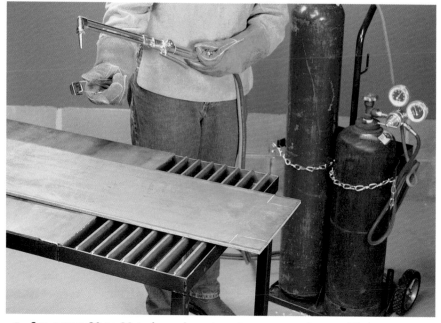

1 See pages 30 to 32 to learn how to set up, pressurize, and light an oxyacetylene torch. Set up the material to be cut on a cutting table. Use soapstone to mark the cutting line, and practice your cutting position and bracing. Hold the torch in your left hand with your thumb and forefinger on the acetylene valve. Hold the striker in your right hand, 3" to 6" from the torch tip. Turn the acetylene valve ¼ to ½ turn and strike sparks.

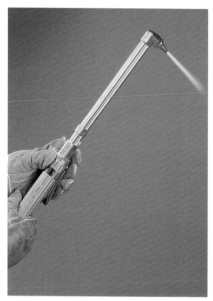

2 Adjust the acetylene so the flame is not smoking and is not separated from the tip (see page 32). Add oxygen to create a neutral flame. With a dedicated cutting torch, depress the oxygen lever to make sure neutral flame is maintained; if necessary, adjust with the oxygen lever depressed. With a cutting tip on a torch base, depress the oxygen lever and use the cutting tip adjustment valve to adjust the oxygen.

3 Release the oxygen lever, flip down your face shield, and direct the flames at the edge of the cut. Once the metal begins to glow red and appears shiny but not yet molten, depress the oxygen lever. If it fails to pierce a hole immediately, release and continue to heat until depressing the lever pierces a hole. Move slowly and steadily along the cutting line, holding the torch at a 90° angle.

4 The finished cut should have very small vertical ridges (draglines), very little slag on the bottom, and the top edges should not be rounded over.

Oxyacetylene Cutting Tips

Piercing Holes and Making Cutouts:

Piercing a hole: Preheat the material to a dull red. Pull back the torch from the surface and angle slightly. Squeeze the oxygen lever. As soon as the material has been pierced, return the torch tip to the perpendicular position and move back to just above the surface. Complete the hole.

Making a cutout: Begin in the center of the cutout and move to the cutout line after piercing a hole. A spiral approach to the edge works best. To give maximum protection to the surrounding material when piercing a hole, drill a ³⁄₁₆" hole to start the piercing action.

Circle cutting guides are available for making accurate circle cuts. If you need to make several circle cutouts, this can be a handy tool.

Oxyacetylene Cutting Safety. Oxyacetylene cutting produces molten slag, sparks, and hot metal scraps. Move items that are to be cut away from burnable material. If the item cannot be moved, protect surrounding areas with sheet metal and fire retardant welding blankets (not tarps). Make sure sparks and slag will not fall into cracks, holes, or ventilation grates in the floor. Wet down any wooden material around the cutting area. Have water, sand, or a fire extinguisher on hand, and monitor the area for one half hour after cutting is completed. Plan where cut metal will fall so it does not hit your arms, legs, gas hoses, or cylinders.

Cutting Defects:

A good oxyacetylene cut has square edges, small vertical draglines, and little slag. A dirty cutting tip is the cause of many poor-quality cuts. Clean the orifices with a properly-sized tip cleaner and use very fine sandpaper on a flat surface to polish the flat surface of the tip. Here are a few possibilities for causes of cutting defects:

Kerf is wider at the bottom than at the top (bell-mouthed).
Oxygen pressure is too high.

Top edge melted over.
Cutting speed is too slow or preheat flames are too long.

Irregular cut edge.
Speed is too fast or too slow, oxygen pressure is too high, or cutting tip is too small or too large.

Use a piece of angle iron as a brace to support the torch or to hold pipe in place for cutting.

WELDING PROJECTS

Here's a chance to put all these welding and cutting techniques to use. The following chapters have directions for creating 23 different projects. Each contains a detailed cutting list, technical drawing, and step-by-step directions.

Among the shop projects you will find a sturdy welding table and a handy welding machine cart. The lighting projects feature a variety of candleholders and lamps. Included in the furniture projects are a delightful wine rack and a handy solution to creating a coffee table out of a slab of stone or wood. The outdoor projects will spark your creativity with an add-your-own-found-objects gate.

SHOP PROJECTS

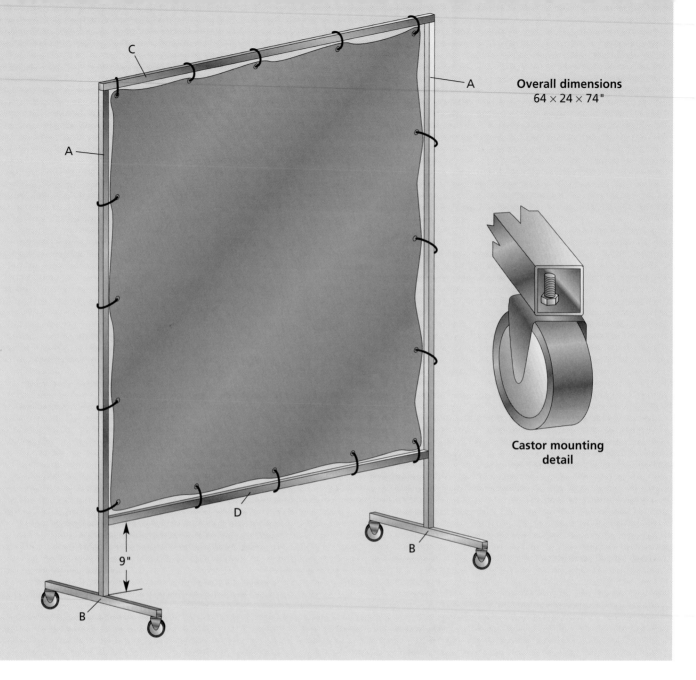

Overall dimensions
64 × 24 × 74"

Castor mounting detail

9"

Rolling Welding Curtain

For arc welding and plasma cutting, it is very important to screen your work area so other shop workers, passersby, family members, and pets are not exposed to the damaging rays. This rolling curtain is quick and easy to make, and it offers the necessary screening while you work. You can purchase ready made welding tarps in a variety of colors, shapes, and sizes (see Resources, page 140). Or you can make your own welding tarp with 12-ounce cotton duck, fire retardant, and grommets.

PART	NAME	DIMENSION	QUANTITY
A	Sides	1 × 1" square tube × 72"	2
B	Wheel supports	1 × 1" square tube × 24"	2
C	Top crossbar	1 × 1" square tube × 64"	1
D	Bottom crossbar	1 × 1" square tube × 62"	1

Sixteen gauge or "thin wall" tube is sufficient for this project.

MATERIALS

- 1 × 1" square tube (27 feet)
- 4 threaded swivel casters, at least one locking
- 5 × 5 foot welding tarp
- Zip ties

How to Build a Rolling Welding Curtain

Attach the Wheel Supports to the Sides

1. Clean all parts with denatured alcohol, acetone, or degreaser. Prepare weld joint areas by wire brushing until shiny.

2. Cut the sides and wheel supports (A & B) to size.

3. Clamp one side piece to the work surface. Center a wheel support at the end of the side piece to form a T.

4. Check for square and tack weld along the butt joint between the two parts. Turn the assembly over and reclamp it to the work surface. Check that the wheel support is still square to the side piece. Make a final weld along the butt joint.

5. Repeat steps 3 and 4 to assemble the second side piece and wheel support.

Weld the Wheel Support T-joints

1. Clamp a side and wheel support assembly to the work surface so the wheel supports hang over the edge.

2. Weld the T-joint between the wheel support and the side piece. Turn the assembly over and weld the second T-joint.

3. Repeat steps 1 to 2 for the second side and wheel support.

Install the Crossbars

1. Cut the top and bottom crossbars (C & D) to size.

2. Place the top crossbar over the side pieces (see photo). Check for square, clamp in place, and tack weld.

3. Make a mark 10" up from the bottom of each wheel support. Align the lower edge of the bottom crossbar with the marks, check for square, and tack in place.

4. Flip the assembly over and check for square by measuring across both diagonals. If the measurements are equal, the structure is square. Clamp the assembly in place and complete the welds. Flip the assembly over and finish the welds on the other side.

Apply Finishing Touches

1. Paint the framework, if desired.

2. Drill holes for the threaded post swivels, ½" from the end of the wheel supports. Install the casters.

3. Attach the tarp to the framework with zip ties.

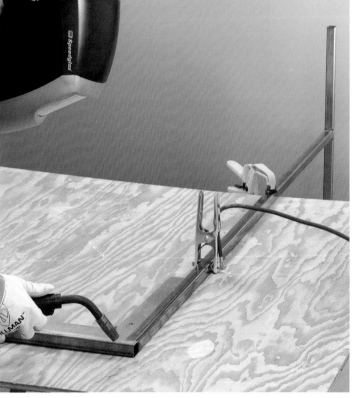

Clamp the sides to the table with the wheel supports hanging over the edge. Finish weld the wheel supports to the sides, then weld the top and bottom crossbars to the sides. Make sure the plywood work surface does not have smoldering embers when you are finished.

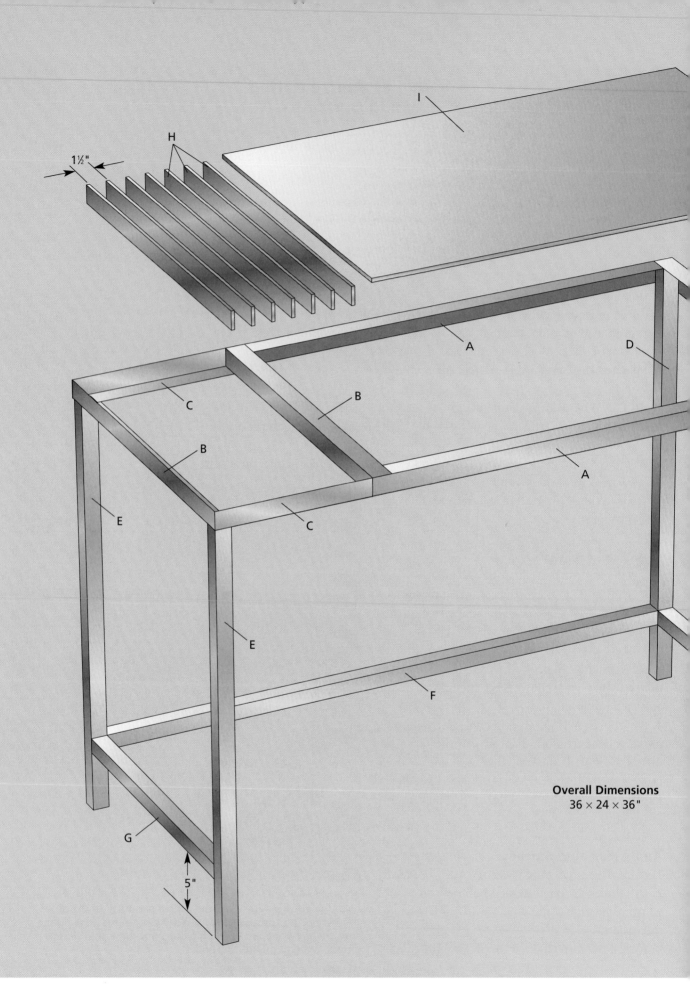

I

H

1½"

A

D

B

C

B

A

E

C

E

F

Overall Dimensions
36 × 24 × 36"

G

5"

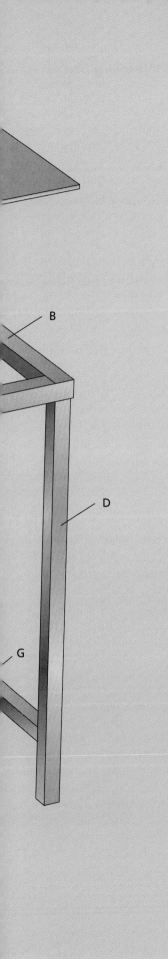

Welding Table

Use it for arc welding, cutting, or oxyfuel welding—this welding table is a versatile addition to your shop. It is sized to allow you to work while sitting on a stool or while standing. You may want to check the scrap bin at the local steel yard to see what size plate steel can be gotten for a reasonable price. Some yards sell plate in 4 foot by 2 foot pre-cut sections that you can cut to size. Or you can have the piece custom cut. You can use material thinner than ³⁄₁₆"—or thicker. Thicker material is better as the table top will have less distortion from the welding heat and the heat generated when you grind spatter off from the table top. You may be able to purchase a small piece of cutting grate; we've constructed our own. Use the sheet metal for the table top on top of sawhorses or a workbench as a work surface to build the rest of the table. You can enclose the area under the cutting table with sheet metal and a door to contain cutting slag and sparks.

PART	NAME	DIMENSIONS	QUANTITY
A	Table top supports (front & back)	⅛ × 1½ × 1½" angle iron × 24"	2
B	Table top supports (sides)	⅛ × 1½ × 1½" angle iron × 24"	3
C	Cutting table supports (front & back)	⅛ × 1½ × 1½" angle iron × 12"	2
D	Right side legs	⅛ × 1¼ × 1¼" square tube × 36"	2
E	Left side legs	⅛ × 1¼ × 1¼" square tube × 34½"	2
F	Stretcher (rear)	⅛ × 1¼ × 1¼" square tube × 36"*	1
G	Stretcher (sides)	⅛ × 1¼ × 1¼" square tube × 21½"*	2
H	Cutting table top	¼ × 1½" flat bar × 23⅞"*	7
I	Table top	³⁄₁₆" sheet metal 24 × 24"	1

*Approximate dimensions, cut to fit

MATERIALS

- ⅛ × 1½ × 1½" angle iron (12 feet)
- ⅛ × 1¼ × 1¼" square tube (19 feet)
- ¼ × 1½" flat bar (14 feet)
- ³⁄₁₆" sheet metal (2 × 2 feet)
- 4 leg levelers

Weld the cutting table section to the table top assembly. The angle iron flange for the table top will face up to support the table top. The angle iron flange for the cutting table will face down to form a well to support the cutting table strips.

How to Build a Welding Table

Weld the Table Top Supports

Cutting notches at the end of the side supports is easier than cutting 45° miters and provides more welding surface area.

1. Cut the table top supports (A & B) and cutting table supports (C) to size. Cut 1½" notches at each end of the three side supports (B) to create a 90° angle joint.

2. Place the table top front support (A) and a table top side support (B) together to form a right angle. Check for square and tack weld.

3. Repeat step 2 using the table top back support and another side support.

4. Assemble these two right angles to make a square. Check all corners for square, and check the assembly for square by measuring both diagonals—they should be equal. If not, adjust the supports so the assembly is square.

5. Complete each outside corner weld, re-checking for square as you go. Flip the assembly over and complete the remaining welds of the joints.

Complete the Table Top Supports

The cutting table supports are positioned with the flange at the bottom to hold the ¼" strips. The table top supports are positioned with the flange at the top to support the table top (see photo, above left).

1. Place the remaining side support (B) and the front and back cutting table supports (C) at right angles to form three sides of a rectangle. Check the corners for square and tack weld the pieces together.

2. Assemble the pieces so the table top supports have the flange at the top, the cutting table supports have the flange at the bottom, and the cutting table supports are abutting the table top supports. Tack weld where the table top sides butt together (see photo, above). Turn the assembly over and weld the remaining joints.

Prepare the Leg Assembly

1. Cut the legs (D & E) to size.

2. Measure the completed table-top. It may be slightly more or less

Place the back stretcher between the right and left side leg assemblies. Make sure the stretcher is square to the legs, then weld in place.

than 24" deep and 36" wide. Adjust the stretcher lengths (F & G) to those measurements, minus the 1¼" for each leg thickness. Cut the stretchers to size.

3. Mark both sets of side legs 5" up from the bottom. Starting with the right side legs (D), place a side stretcher (G) between the legs with the bottom of the stretcher aligned with the 5" mark.

4. Align the stretcher at a 90° angle to the side legs and clamp the assembly to your work surface. Tack weld the top inside angle at each end of the stretcher.

5. Repeat this process for the left side legs.

Finish the Leg Assembly

1. Place the leg assemblies on their sides with the rear side down, and clamp to your work surface.

2. Position the rear stretcher (F) between the right and left leg assemblies, aligning the bottom of the stretcher with the 5" mark.

3. Align the stretcher at a 90° angle to the assemblies and clamp in place. Tack weld the inside angles (see photo, below left).

Assemble the Table

The right legs fit inside the corner made by the angle iron, while the left legs are set back ⅛" from the edges of the angle iron.

1. Turn the table top and cutting table assembly upside down, then set the leg assembly into it.

2. Clamp the pieces in place. Check for square on both sides, front, and back.

3. Tack weld all corners. Check for square again, then weld all pieces into place.

Tack weld grating strips to the angle iron every 1½" to form the cutting table top.

Install the Cutting Table Top

Tack welding the cutting table grating allows you to remove and replace the ¼" strips as they become worn from the cutting torch.

1. Cut the cutting table top grating (H) to size.

2. Place a strip of grating into the well formed by the cutting table top supports, 1½" from the table top edge.

3. Tack weld the top edge of the grating to the angle iron.

4. Place another grating strip 1½" from the first strip and tack weld in place. Continue building the cutting table top in this manner until complete (see photo, above).

5. Grind down the welds on the top of the table top support assembly.

Finish the Table

1. Place the table top (I) onto the assembly and tack weld twice on each side.

2. Weld the table top to the supports using 1" or 2" weld beads at both sides of each corner and twice along each side.

3. Grind down the welds, if desired. Wire brush, sand, or sandblast the entire table.

4. Paint the table, but do not paint the table top or cutting grate.

5. Install leg levelers as needed.

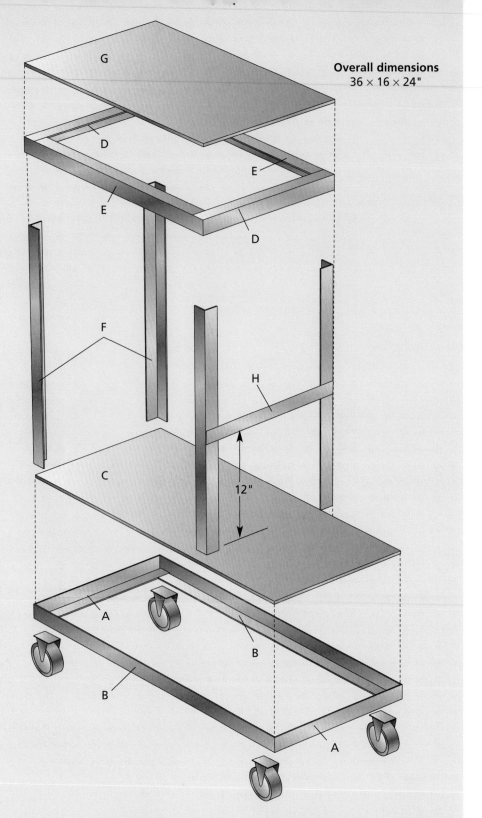

Overall dimensions
36 × 16 × 24"

Welding Machine Cart

You'll want a cart for your GMAW or GTAW machine and gas cylinder—why not build it as your first project? It's good practice, and the materials will cost much less than most commercial carts. If you keep your eyes open, you can probably pick up the angle iron for free the next time a neighbor throws away an old bedframe. Remember, however, to grind off the paint at the joints, otherwise you'll have nasty fumes and poor quality welds.

Include a rubber pad and insulated chain for the gas cylinder (not shown) so an arc can't accidentally be struck against the cylinder.

MATERIALS

- ⅛ × 1½ × 1½" angle iron (24 feet)
- ⅛" sheet metal (3 × 3 feet)
- ⅛ × 1¼" flat bar (16")
- Swivel casters (4)
- Eyebolts (2)
- Chain (2 feet)
- Threaded chain links (2)
- Rubber pad (10 × 16")
- Rubber tubing (2 feet)

PART	NAME	DIMENSIONS	QUANTITY
A	Bottom front & back	⅛ × 1½ × 1½" angle iron × 16"	2
B	Bottom sides	⅛ × 1½ × 1½" angle iron × 36"	2
C	Tray	⅛" sheet × 16 × 36"*	1
D	Top front & back	⅛ × 1½ × 1½" angle iron × 16"	2
E	Top sides	⅛ × 1½ × 1½" angle iron × 26"	2
F	Legs	⅛ × 1½ × 1½" angle iron × 24"	4
G	Top	⅛" sheet × 16 × 26"*	1
H	Brace	⅛ × 1¼" flat bar × 16"	1

*Approximate dimensions, cut to fit

How to Build a Welding Machine Cart

Assemble the Base & Tray

1. Cut the bottom front and back (A) to size. Cut the bottom side pieces (B) to size. Instead of mitering the corners, cut a 1½" notch at each end (see diagram).

2. Arrange the front, back, and side pieces to form a rectangle. Check the corners for square, clamp in place, and tack weld the pieces together.

3. Measure diagonally across the corners to make sure they are square. If the measurements are equal, the base is square. If they are not, adjust the pieces until they are.

4. Clamp the base in place. Weld each outside corner. Turn the base over and weld each joint. Do not weld inside the base, as the weld beads will interfere with the tray and leg placement.

5. Measure the inside dimensions of the base and cut the tray (C) to size.

6. Insert the tray into the angles of the base. Tack weld the tray at points along the perimeter.

7. Turn the assembly over and place three 1" welds along each long side, and two 1" welds along each short side to join the tray to the base.

Assemble the Top

1. Cut the top front and back (D) and top side pieces (E) to size. Cut a 1½" notch at each end of the side pieces.

2. Arrange the front, back, and side pieces to form a rectangle. Check the corners for square, clamp in place, and tack weld the pieces together.

3. Measure diagonally across the corners to make sure they are square. If the measurements are equal, the top assembly is square. If they are not, adjust the pieces until they are.

4. Clamp the pieces in place. Weld each outside corner. Turn the assembly over and weld each joint. Do not weld inside the top assembly, as the weld beads will interfere with the top and leg placement.

5. Measure the top assembly to allow a ⅛" setback on all sides, and cut the top (G) to size.

6. Grind down the welds and place the top over the assembly. Tack weld the top along the perimeter, then finish weld with two 1" welds per side.

Attach the Legs

1. Cut the legs (F) and brace (H) to size.

2. Turn the top upside down. Place a leg in one of the corners. Use a scrap piece of angle iron to assist in clamping (see photo). Make sure the leg is square to the top and tack weld into place.

3. Repeat step 2 to attach the other three legs to the corners of the top.

4. Place the legs and top assembly into the bottom assembly. The back legs should fit into the corners of the bottom assembly, and the front legs into the angles of the side pieces of the base.

5. Make sure the legs are square to the base, clamp, and tack weld.

6. Measure across the diagonals between the base and the top to make sure the unit is square. Adjust, if necessary, and finish welding the legs to the top and base.

7. Measure 12" from the bottom of the front legs Center the brace over the marks, check it for square, and clamp in place. Weld the brace to the front legs.

Add Finishing Touches

1. Sand and clean the cart, and paint.

2. Drill holes 2" in from the ends of the brace and attach the eyebolts. Use the threaded chain links to attach the chain.

3. Turn the cart over. Grind down the welds at the corners and attach the casters. If you are welding the casters, make sure you grind off the zinc coating.

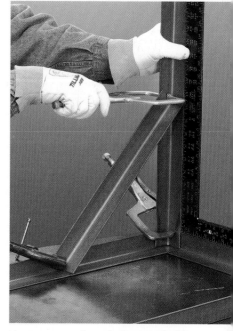

Use a scrap of angle iron to hold the legs in place for tacking.

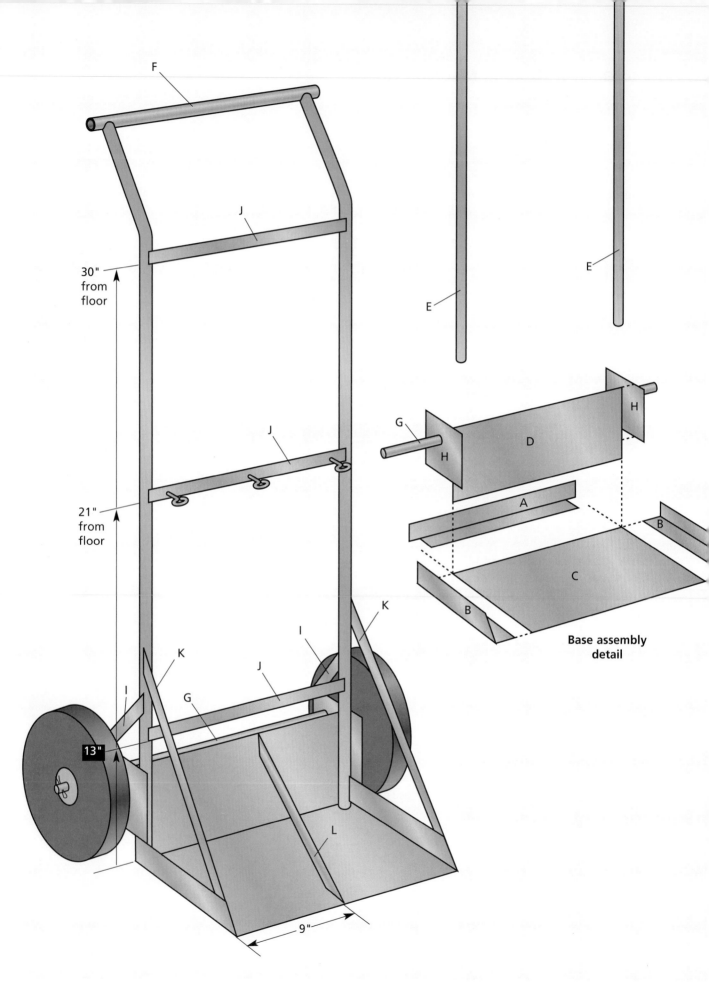

F

J

30"
from
floor

J

21"
from
floor

K

I

G

K

I

J

K

13"

L

9"

G

H

D

H

E

E

E

A

B

C

B

B

**Base assembly
detail**

Cylinder Cart

You can purchase a cylinder cart for your oxyfuel rig—your dealer might even give you a discount—but it's fun and challenging to make your own. This cart is constructed with ⅛" stock, which is oxyfuel weldable, but we used GMAW. The base platform and back support can be flame or plasma cut. If you have access to a heavy-duty metal brake, you can make the base platform and back support from one 16¼ × 17¾" piece and bend it to 90° (allow ¼" for the radius of the bend).

PART	NAME	DIMENSIONS	QUANTITY
A	Base back	⅛ × 1½ × 1½" angle iron × 18"	1
B	Base sides	⅛ × 1½ × 1½" angle iron ×10"	2
C	Base platform	⅛" sheet × 10 × 17¾"*	1
D	Back support	⅛" sheet × 6 × 17¾"*	1
E	Handle uprights	⅛ × 1" round tube × 60"*	2
F	Handle	⅛ × 1" round tube × 18"	1
G	Axle	⅝" round bar × 22"*	1
H	Axle brackets	⅛" sheet × 4 × 4½"	2
I	Bracket supports	⅛ × 1½" flat bar × 8"*	2
J	Crosspieces	⅛ × 1½" flat bar × 17"*	3
K	Side supports	⅛ × 1¼" flat bar × 24"*	2
L	Base support	⅛ × 1½" flat bar × 12"*	1

*Approximate dimensions, cut to fit

MATERIALS

- ⅛ × 1½ × 1½" angle iron (3½ feet)
- ⅛" sheet metal (18 × 24" sheet)
- ⅛ × 1" round tube (12 feet)
- ⅝" round bar (2 feet)
- ⅛ × 1½" flat bar (7 feet)
- ⅛ × 1¼" flat bar (4 feet)
- 1" eyebolts with nuts (3)
- Chain
- Snap closures or threaded chain links (3)
- 8" wheels with hubs (2)
- Washers and cotter pins (2)

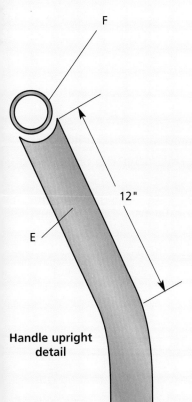

F

12"

E

**Handle upright
detail**

How to Build a Cylinder Cart

Prepare the Cart Base

1. Cut the base back (A) and base sides (B) to size. Rather than mitering the corners, cut a 1½" notch in each end of the base back (see diagram).

2. Mark and cut a triangular section off the front end of each base side to soften the edge.

3. Lay out the base back and sides to form a three sided rectangle. Square the corners and clamp the assembly to your work surface.

4. Tack the joints at both ends of the base back. Turn the assembly over and weld the corner and butt joints.

After welding the base back and sides, cut the base platform and back support to fit, then weld them in place.

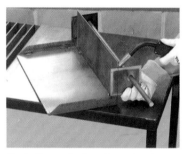

Tack the axle brackets to the base assembly. Insert the axle to check for proper alignment, then finish weld the bracket joints.

Install the Base Platform & Back Support

1. Measure the inside width of the base assembly and cut the base platform (C) and back support (D) to size.

2. Place the base platform into the base assembly and tack weld it into place along the base sides.(Do not weld along the base back, as that would prevent the back support from fitting flat against the base platform.)

3. Turn the base over and place two 1" welds along each side where the base platform meets the back and sides.

4. Set the base flat on the work surface, right side up, and place the back support upright against the inside of the base back (see photo, above).

5. Clamp the back support to the base back. Place three 1" welds on the back side of the support where it meets the angle iron.

6. Place two 1" welds on the inside T-joint, making sure not to weld within two inches of the corner.

Attach the Axle Brackets

1. Cut the axle brackets (H) to size.

2. Place the base assembly on its side and align an axle bracket along the top edge of the base side, resting it on top of the back support and extending 3" off the back side.

3. Measure 4" up from the bottom of the base assembly and 1½" from the back edge to mark the axle location on the axle bracket. Drill, flame cut, or plasma cut a ⅝" hole at the mark.

4. Tack weld the axle bracket in place (see photo, above left). Insert the axle to check for proper alignment, then weld both sides of the T-joint between the bracket and the back support.

5. Weld the outside butt joint between the bracket and the base side.

6. Repeat steps 2 to 5 to weld an axle bracket to the other side of the base assembly.

Prepare the Handle Uprights

1. Cut the handle uprights (E) to length.

2. Make a 20° to 30° bend in one of the handle uprights, 13" from one end, using a heavy-duty conduit bender. Bend the other handle upright to match.

3. Cut both pieces so the curve is 12" from the top end and the overall upright height of each is 48". Grind the tops of both handle uprights so they fit around the handle tube.

Assemble & Install Handle Uprights

1. Place a handle upright against the inside corner of the base assembly. Turn the handle so the curve points straight back. Tack weld the handle in place. Repeat this process for the other handle upright.

2. Cut the handle (F) to size.

3. Place the cart on its back. Set the handle against the cutouts in the handle uprights, keeping an equal amount of overhang on each end, and tack weld in place.

4. Finish weld the handle uprights to the base assembly. Place welds between the handle uprights and top back support, and between the handle uprights and axle brackets.

Attach the Crosspieces

1. Measure and cut the crosspieces (J) so they are slightly recessed against the handle uprights.

2. Drill three ³⁄₁₆" holes—one in the center and one on each end of one crosspiece. Place this crosspiece 21" up from the base.

3. Set the remaining crosspieces at 13" and 30" from the base on the forward side of the handle uprights, and weld in place (see photo, right).

Attach the Supports

1. Turn the assembly on its side. Place a bracket support (I) in position across the handle upright and the axle bracket. Mark the angles on the support and cut it to size.

2. Weld the bracket support in place against the handle upright and axle bracket.

3. Set the side support (K) in position against the base side and the handle upright. Mark the angles and cut to fit. Weld the support in place.

4. Turn the assembly on its opposite side and repeat steps 1 to 3.

5. Mark the angles and cut the base support (L) to size to fit between the base platform and the base back.

6. Center the base support from side to side on the base assembly. Weld both sides of each T-joint.

Lay the crosspieces across the handle uprights at the proper heights. Weld the pieces to the uprights.

Complete the Cart

1. Center the axle (G) between the axle brackets. Place the wheels on the axle to make sure the wheels barely make contact with the floor (see photo, right).

2. Mark the axle for its final length and cut to size. Drill holes in each end of the axle to fit the cotter pins.

3. Center the axle between the axle brackets and weld in place.

4. Complete any unfinished welds.

5. Wire brush or sandblast the cart. Clean the cart and paint as desired.

6. Attach the wheels to the axle. Insert cotter pins in the axle holes.

7. Affix eyebolts with nuts in the 3 holes in the middle crosspiece. Attach the chain to the eyebolts with snap closures or threaded chain links.

Trial fit the wheels before welding the axle into place. The wheels should just barely make contact with the floor.

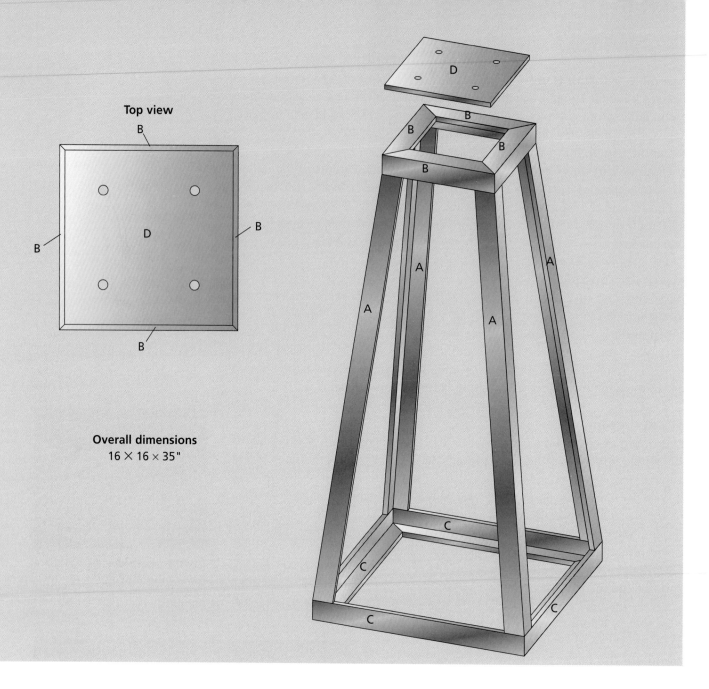

Top view

Overall dimensions
16 × 16 × 35"

Grinder Stand

This is a good project to make with angle iron from the discount bin at the local steel supply center. You can often buy short pieces for 10 cents a pound rather than the 30 to 50 cents you would normally pay. Take along your calipers or micrometer to measure thicknesses, as well as your measuring tape, cutting list, and tough gloves so you don't get cut digging through the scrap pile.

PART	NAME	DIMENSIONS	QUANTITY
A	Legs	³⁄₁₆ × 1½ × 1½" angle iron × 32"	4
B	Top	³⁄₁₆ × 1½ × 1½" angle iron × 8½"	4
C	Bottom	³⁄₁₆ × 1½ × 1½" angle iron × 16"	4
D	Platform	³⁄₁₆ to ½" plate 8 × 8"	1

MATERIALS

- ³⁄₁₆ × 1½ × 1½" angle iron (19 feet)
- ³⁄₁₆" plate (8 × 8")

How to Build a Grinder Stand

Build the Top & Bottom Assemblies

1. Cut the top and bottom pieces (B & C) to length. Miter the corners at 45° or cut 1½" notches into the pieces.

2. Assemble pairs of bottom pieces into right angles. Clamp the pieces to your work surface and tack weld at each corner.

3. Assemble the two right angles into a square. Check for square by measuring across each diagonal—if the measurements are equal, the assembly is square. Tack weld the corners.

4. Repeat steps 2 to 3 to assemble the top.

Mark & Cut the Legs

1. Cut the legs (A) to size.

2. Place the bottom assembly on your work surface and loosely clamp the legs into each corner.

3. Set the top assembly over the legs and clamp it in place. Make sure the top is level.

4. Mark each leg at the top and bottom where they cross the platforms (see photo).

5. Unclamp the legs and cut to size.

Assemble the Stand

1. Place one leg on top of a corner of the bottom assembly and tack weld it in place. Tack weld the other three legs in the corners the same way.

2. Align a corner of the top assembly with the top of one leg and tack it in place. Tack weld the top assembly to the other three legs the same way.

3. Adjust the stand so the top is level. You may need to remove tack welds and grind down some angles.

4. When you are satisfied with the alignment, complete the welds. To minimize distortion, alternate between the sides, top, and bottom as you weld.

Attach the Platform Plate

1. Cut the platform plate (D) to size. Drill four holes in the face to match your grinder mounting holes.

2. Set the plate over the top of the stand, aligning the edges with the outside of the top pieces. Weld the plate to the stand.

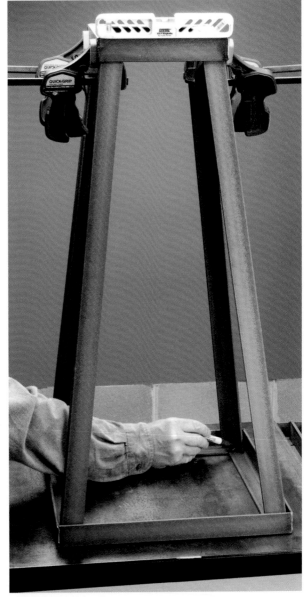

Assemble the grinder stand using clamps. Mark the top and bottom of each leg and cut to fit.

LIGHTING PROJECTS

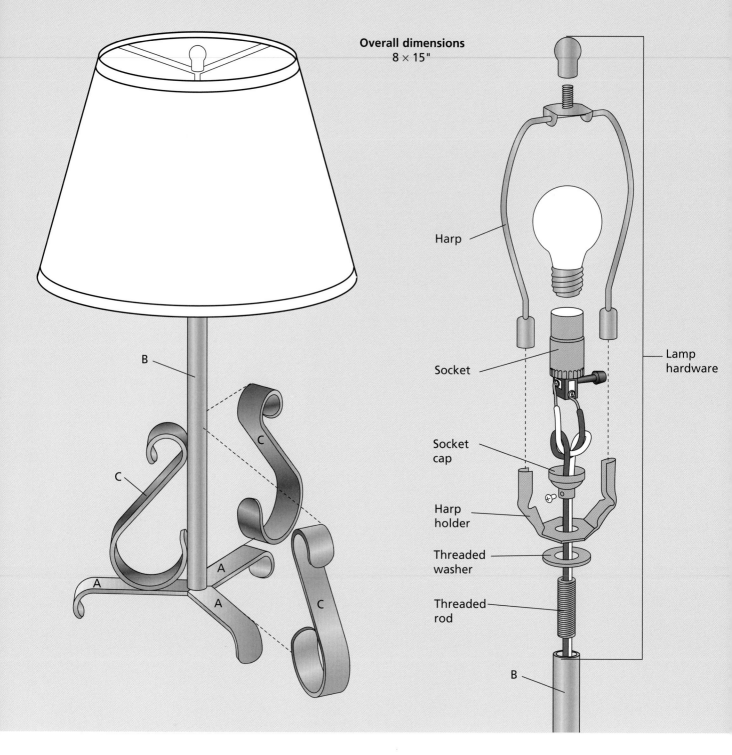

Overall dimensions
8 × 15"

Harp

Socket

Lamp
hardware

Socket
cap

Harp
holder

Threaded
washer

Threaded
rod

B

B

C

C

A

A

A

Scroll Desk Lamp

In this project, you will make simple scrolls—or you can purchase wrought iron scrolls from a wrought iron supplier or blacksmith. (See Metal Shaping Techniques, page 19, or Resources, page 140.) Either way, this makes a delightful little desk lamp.

PART	NAME	DIMENSIONS	QUANTITY
A	Bases	⅛ × ¾" flat bar × 5"	3
B	Shaft	½" round tube × 9"	1
C	Scrolls	⅛ × ½" flat bar × 12"	3

How to Make a Scroll Desk Lamp

Assemble the Base

1. Cut the base pieces (A) and shaft (B) to size.

2. Round one end of each base piece using a bench or angle grinder. Clamp the rounded ends to a ½" pipe. Curl the ends to form an arc.

3. Turn the base pieces upside down and arrange them so they are equally spaced at the 12, 4, and 8 o'clock positions (120° between adjacent pieces at their centerlines).

4. Use a grinder to shape the flat end on each base piece to fit against the other two legs. Once the pieces are fitted, center the ½" tube on the arranged pieces and mark around the tube.

5. Grind the legs so the tube fits in the shaped opening, but don't insert the shaft at this time.

6. Tack weld the undersides of the legs at each contact point.

Attach the Tube

1. Turn the base assembly right side up and insert the tube. Check for square and tack weld at three points.

2. Check for square again, adjust the pieces if necessary, and complete the weld around the base of the tube. (You can weld the tube from the bottom side only, but a solid weld all around the top looks nice.)

Prepare & Attach Scrolls

1. Cut the scrolls (C) to size.

2. Round both ends of the scroll pieces with a grinder.

3. Using a 1" pipe, make a 1" circle at one end of each scroll. Using a 2" pipe, make a 2" circle at the other end of the scrolls, facing the opposite direction. (Because of the springiness of the steel, the final circles will be slightly larger.)

4. Place one scroll against the base and the shaft, arranging it in a pleasing manner. Tack weld it in place where it touches the base and shaft.

5. Place and tack weld the second and third scrolls, taking care to align them carefully. When satisfied with the placement and alignment, tack weld on the opposite sides of the scrolls (see photo).

Apply Finishing Touches

1. Clean up the welds, and apply the finish of your choice.

2. Tap threads in the top of the shaft (or weld a small nut to the top of the shaft), and insert the hollow threaded rod. Thread the wire through the shaft and rod. Thread the washer, and place the harp holder over the threaded rod. Screw on the socket cap, and tighten the set screw. Wire the fixture (see diagram). Press the socket assembly into the socket cap, place the harp in the harp holder, and install the lightbulb and shade.

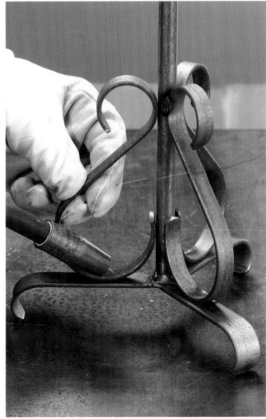

Arrange the scrolls against the base and shaft, then weld the scrolls in place on both sides.

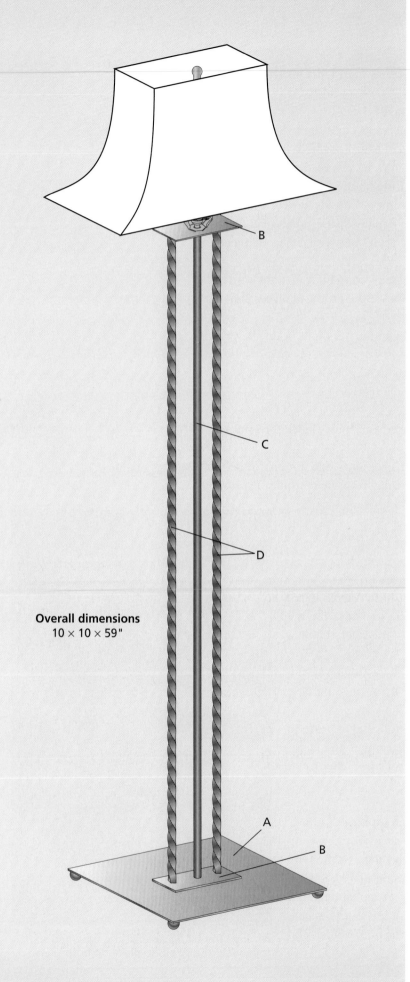

Overall dimensions
10 × 10 × 59"

Three Post Floor Lamp

A welded lamp has a nice heft to it—with this 10" square base, it will be difficult to tip, no doubt! We used fully twisted rod because it creates a simple contrast of square twists and smooth rounds and is available in longer lengths. Partially twisted rod is also available. You also could use any of a variety of decorative hammered square bars or tubes from the sources listed in the Resource section on page 140. While you're making a floor lamp, you could make a desk lamp to match. Just adjust the dimensions to fit.

PART	NAME	DIMENSIONS	QUANTITY
A	Base	³⁄₁₆" sheet 10 × 10"	1
B	End caps	³⁄₁₆" flat bar 2 × 4"	2
C	Center post	½" round tube 48⅜"	1
D	Side posts	½" twisted rod 48"	2

MATERIALS

- ½" round tube (48⅜")
- ½" twisted square rod (96")
- ³⁄₁₆" sheet (10 × 10")
- ³⁄₁₆ × 2" flat bar (8")
- 1" round balls (4)
- Lamp hardware and shade

How to Make a Three Post Floor Lamp

Prepare the Work Pieces

1. Cut the end caps (B) to size. Cut the center post (C) and side posts (D) to size.

2. Mark the end caps at ¾", 2", and 3¼" from one end. Make a mark lengthwise through the center of each end cap.

3. At the intersection of the 2" and the centerline marks in each end cap, drill a ½" diameter hole.

Attach the Center Post to the End Caps

1. Insert the center post into the hole in one of the end caps. Check the post for square, then tack weld the post at the bottom.

2. Repeat step 1 to tack weld the other end cap onto the opposite end of the center post.

3. Stand the center post and end caps upright and carefully weld around the post.

Attach the Side Posts

1. Place the lamp assembly flat on your work surface. Center a side post over the ¾" mark on one of the end caps. Check the post for square and tack weld in place.

2. Place the side post in position on the second end cap. Check for square and tack weld.

3. Repeat steps 1 and 2 to attach the second side post to the end caps at the 3¼" marks.

4. Square all the parts and complete each weld all around each post and end cap (see photo).

Attach the Post Assembly to the Base

1. Cut the base (A) to size.

2. Make a line 3" in from each side of the base and 4" in from the top and bottom. Draw lines at 5" lengthwise and widthwise to mark the center point.

3. Drill a ½" diameter hole at the center of the base for the cord.

4. Weld a 1" ball ½" from the edges at each corner of the base for the feet.

5. Turn the base right side up. Clamp the post assembly to the base, centering the base on the lines marked in step 2. The holes for the cord should line up. If not, enlarge the hole in the base.

6. Tack weld the post assembly to the base on two sides. Check for square. Complete the fillet weld around the base. Weld toward the tack points to minimize distortion.

Apply Finishing Touches

1. Grind down any spatter or uneven welds. Apply the finish of your choice.

2. Tap threads in the top of the shaft (or weld a small nut to the top of the shaft), and insert the hollow threaded rod. Thread the wire through the shaft and rod. Place the washer and harp holder over the threaded rod. Screw on the socket cap, and tighten the set screw. Wire the fixture (see diagram, page 92). Press the socket assembly into the socket cap, place the harp in the harp holder, and install the lightbulb and shade.

Make sure the posts are square to the end caps, then weld them in place.

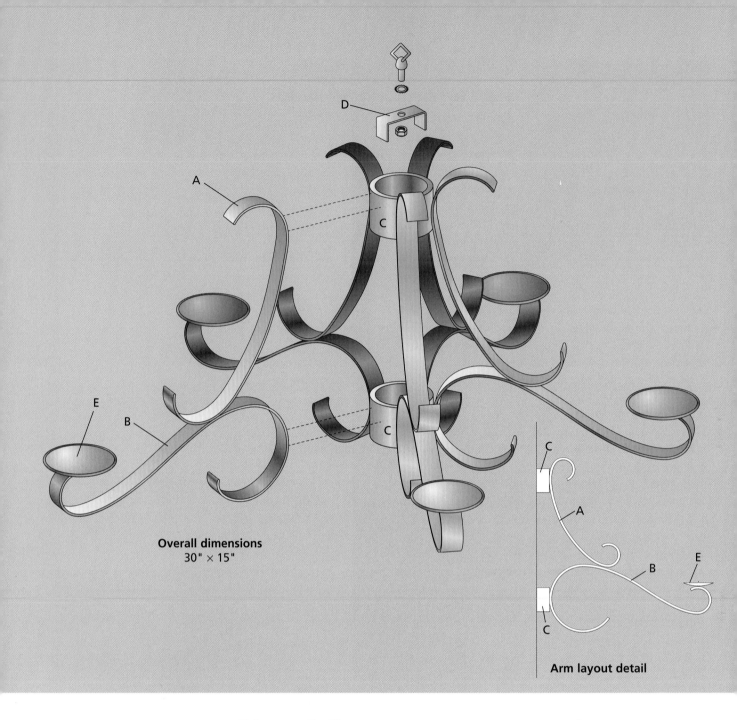

Overall dimensions
30" × 15"

Arm layout detail

Chandelier

This delightful candle chandelier is a wonderful accent for cabins, porches, or even outside dining. Making the scrolls is easy, but if you want something a bit fancier, you can purchase wrought iron scrolls. Place the scrolls carefully around the couplers to ensure the fixture will hang straight. If you do not want to purchase a long section of round tube for two 2" pieces and can't find any in the scrap bin at the steel yard, use threaded black pipe couplers.

PART	NAME	DIMENSIONS	QUANTITY
A	C scrolls	⅛ × ¾" flat bar × 16"	5
B	S scrolls	⅛ × ¾" flat bar × 24"	5
C	Couplers	2¼" round tube × 2"	2
D	Insert	⅛ × ¾" flat bar × 4"	1
E	Bobeches	2½"	5

MATERIALS

- ⅛ × ¾" flat bar (17 feet)
- 10", 6", 2", and 1" bending forms
- 2¼" round tube (4")
- 2½" bobeches (5)
- 2" threaded nipple
- Lock washers (2)
- Threaded brass washers (3)
- Finial
- Decorative chain
- Candles (5)

How to Make a Chandelier

Prepare the C Scroll Blanks

1. Cut the C scroll (A) and S scroll (B) blanks to size.

2. Clamp a C scroll blank to the 10" bending form. Shape the entire length of the scroll blank. Lightly tap the scroll with a hammer, if necessary, to get it to conform.

3. Remove the scroll from the form. Reclamp one end of the scroll to the 1" form and shape that end into a tight curve. Repeat this step to shape the opposite end.

4. Repeat steps 2 and 3 to shape the remaining C scrolls.

Prepare the S Scroll Blanks

1. Mark each S scroll blank 9½" from one end. Clamp the marked end to the 6" bending form.

2. Wrap the bar around the form, shaping it just past the mark.

3. Clamp that same end to the 2" form. Wrap the bar almost all the way around the form.

4. Unwrap the large curve slightly, refining the scroll into a pleasing shape.

5. To curve the other end in the opposite direction, turn the piece over and clamp it to the 2" form. Wrap the bar almost all the way around.

Assemble the Scrolls

1. Set a straightedge on a large piece of paper. Lay out one C scroll and one S scroll along the straightedge, and adjust them until they form a pleasing shape. Mark the contact point on the bars.

2. Remove the scrolls from the paper and weld them together at the contact point.

3. Trace the outline of this assembly on the paper (see photo, top right). Use this pattern to arrange and assemble the remaining arms.

Assemble the Chandelier

1. Cut the couplers (C) and insert (D) to length.

2. Drill a hole in the center of the insert large enough for the threaded nipple. Bend tabs on each end of the insert so it will fit inside a coupler.

3. Place the insert into a coupler, with the tabs pointing down. Weld the insert to the coupler along the tabs. This forms the top coupler.

4. Draw a line around the outside of each coupler on paper.

5. Mark five equidistant points around the coupler outline. Place the coupler back on the paper and transfer the lines onto the coupler, using a combination square (see photo, bottom right).

6. Weld the arms to the couplers. Weld the bobeches to the arms.

Apply Finishing Touches

1. Place a lock washer and threaded brass washer on the threaded nipple. Set this in the hole in the insert and secure it with another lock washer and threaded brass washer.

2. Add a threaded brass washer and a finial.

3. Wire brush and clean the chandelier. Apply your choice of finish.

4. Clip the chain into the finial, and it's ready to hang.

After welding the first set of scrolls, trace the outline on a sheet of paper. Use this pattern to arrange the remaining scrolls.

Use a combination square to mark the arm placement on each coupler.

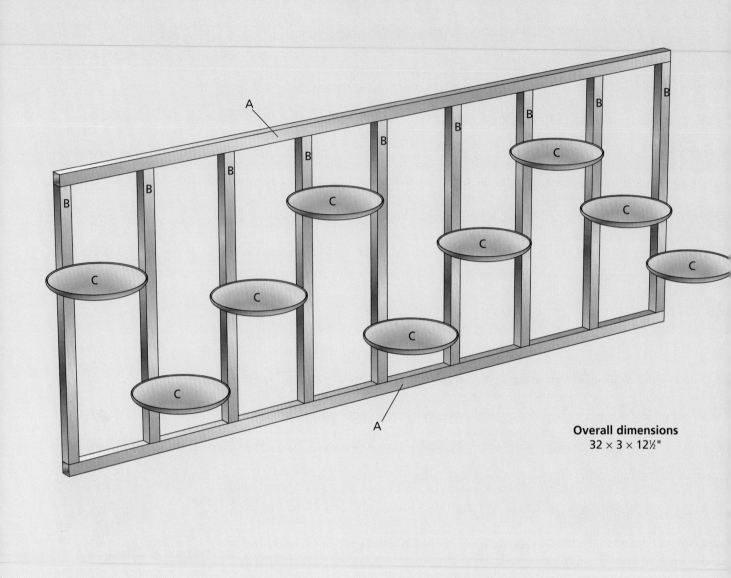

Overall dimensions
32 × 3 × 12½"

Wall-mounted Candleholder

This wall-mounted candleholder is perfect for a patio wall or over a buffet table. The length and height can be adjusted easily to suit your particular wall space. Or it easily can be turned to run vertically rather than horizontally. Candle drip trays, or bobeches, do not have holes, while bobeches for electrical fixtures do. See Resources, page 140, for bobeche sources. Clean all weld areas prior to welding. When hanging the candleholder, use hangers rated to hold 25 pounds. (The holder will weigh about 13 pounds, plus candles. Remember never to leave burning candles unattended.)

PART	NAME	DIMENSIONS	QUANTITY
A	Horizontal bars	½" square bar × 32"	2
B	Vertical bars	½" square bar × 11½"	9
C	Bobeches	2¼"	9

How to Build a Wall mounted Candleholder

Assemble the Horizontal & Vertical Bars

1. Cut the horizontal (A) and vertical (B) bars to length.

2. Butt a vertical bar against the inside left edge of the top horizontal bar. Use a framing square to ensure the pieces are set at a 90° angle. Tack weld the inside of the angle.

3. Butt another vertical bar against the inside right end of the bottom horizontal bar. Make sure the angle is 90° and tack weld on the inside.

4. Place the two angled pieces together to make a rectangle, with the vertical bars on the inside of the horizontal bars. Use the framing square to adjust the angles to 90° and clamp in place.

5. Measure diagonally across the corners. If the measurements are the same, the piece is square. If not, adjust the bars so the measurements are equal.

6. Tack the two corners, and check again for square. Weld all four outside corners.

Attach the Vertical Bars

1. Place the remaining vertical bars at 4" intervals between the end pieces. Make sure the spacing is even, then mark where each vertical piece should go.

2. Check each piece for square and weld in place.

Attach the Bobeches

1. Place the bobeches (C) on the vertical bars in a pleasingly staggered pattern.

2. Clean the edge of each bobeche and the areas on the bars where they will be placed to ensure a good weld.

3. Use a magnetic clamp to hold the bobeche at a right angle to the bar and weld from the top side (see photo). When welding, direct most of the heat toward the bar since it is much thicker than the bobeche.

4. Remove the clamp. Make sure the bobeche still meets the vertical bar at a right angle and is level from side to side. Weld the bobeche from the bottom side.

5. Repeat steps 3 to 4 to attach the remaining bobeches.

Apply Finishing Touches

1. Grind down the welds for a smooth look.

2. Finish the piece as desired. A rusted metal finish is appropriately rustic for outdoor use.

Place the bobeche at a right angle to the vertical bar using a magnetic clamp. Weld the bobeche in place, directing most of the heat toward the bar.

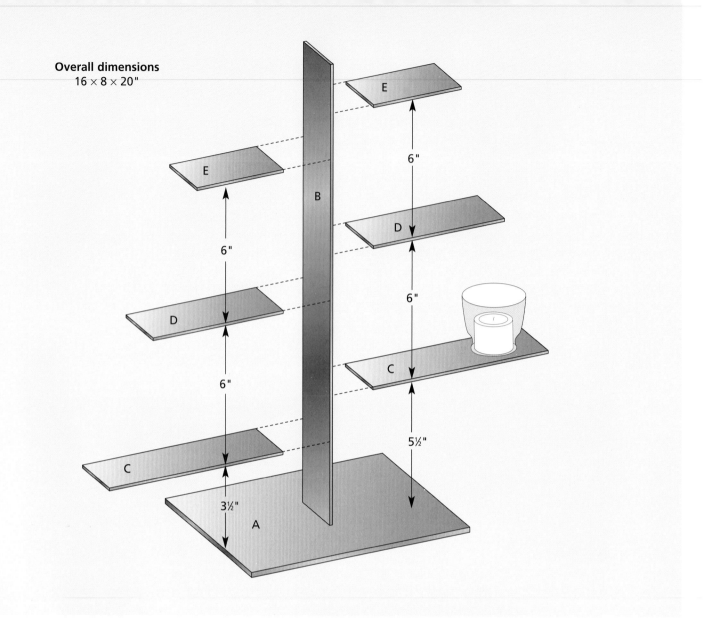

Overall dimensions
16 × 8 × 20"

Tree-shaped Candleholder

This tree-shaped candleholder displays an assortment of votive candles. The tree shape is also handy as a photo display area, if you aren't interested in a candleholder. An option is to use square tubing and make a four-sided tree—perhaps even a larger version as a dramatic substitute for a Christmas tree. Most steel supply shops have pre-cut squares of steel sheet and plate in a variety of sizes. A smaller, thicker base would be just as stable. You may opt to make the base round and give the tree trunk a pointed top, if you will be cutting your own pieces. Some steel distributors and welding shops do custom shearing. (Remember not to leave burning candles unattended.)

PART	NAME	DIMENSIONS	QUANTITY
A	Base	³⁄₁₆" sheet × 8 × 10"	1
B	Trunk	³⁄₁₆ × 2" flat bar × 20"	1
C	Bottom branches	³⁄₁₆ × 2" flat bar × 8"	2
D	Middle branches	³⁄₁₆ × 2" flat bar × 6"	2
E	Top branches	³⁄₁₆ × 2" flat bar × 4"	2

How to Make a Tree-shaped Candleholder

Assemble the Trunk

1. Cut the base (A), trunk (B), and branches (C, D, & E) to size.

2. Place the trunk upright in the center of the base, parallel to the 8" sides of the base. Clamp the trunk at a 90° angle to the base using a magnetic clamp.

3. Tack weld the trunk at each end on both sides.

4. Remove the clamp. Make sure the trunk is still square, then complete the welds.

Attach the Branches

1. Place the bottom branch 3½" up from the base and magnetically clamp it in place at a 90° angle to the trunk.

2. Tack weld the branch to the trunk at each end on the top side (see photo).

3. Remove the clamp and complete the weld.

4. Place the second bottom branch on the opposite side of the trunk, 5½" from the base. Weld in place.

5. Repeat the process by setting the middle branches 9½" and 11½" from the base, and the top branches 15½" and 17½" from the base.

Apply Finishing Touches

1. Clean the metal and the welds with a wire brush.

2. Finish the candleholder as desired.

3. Use silicone adhesive to attach a votive holder to the end of each branch if desired.

A right angle magnetic clamp makes welding the branches an easy task.

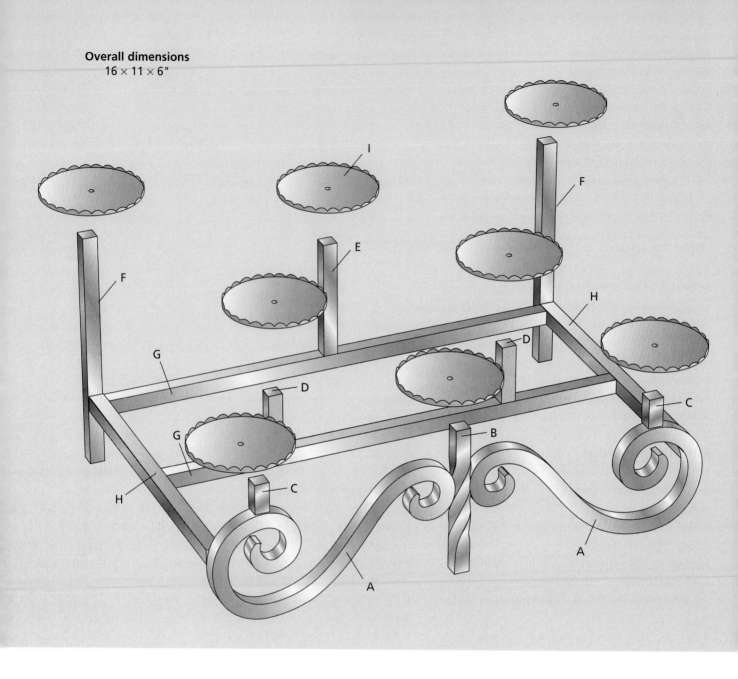

Fireplace Candleholder

In the summertime, place this candleholder in your fireplace to enjoy flickering flames of firelight without the heat of the fire. This project uses forged scrolls, but you can bend your own, if you wish.

PART	NAME	DIMENSIONS	QUANTITY
A	Scrolls	4 × 8"	2
B	Center post	½" twisted square rod × 5"	1
C	Front extenders	½" square rod × 1"	2
D	Middle extenders	½" square rod × 2"	2
E	Rear extender	½" square rod × 3"	1
F	Rear posts	½" square rod × 6"	2
G	Crosspieces	½" square rod × 16"*	2
H	Side pieces	½" square rod × 10"	2
I	Bobeches	3⅜"	8

*Approximate dimensions, cut to fit

How to Build a Fireplace Candleholder

Assemble the Scrolls

1. Cut the center post (B) to size.

2. Place the scrolls (A) on their sides with the small circles butted against the center post. (If the scroll ends have been hammered out to form a flared end, you will need to use shims to make the pieces lie flat.)

3. Clamp the workpieces to your work surface, and weld the scrolls to the center post.

Assemble the Holder Base

1. Measure the length of the two scrolls and center post, and subtract 1". Cut the crosspieces (G) to this length.

2. Cut the rear posts (F) and side pieces (H) to size.

3. Place the crosspieces between the side pieces; one at one end and one in the middle. Weld the crosspieces in place.

4. Mark 2" up from the bottom of the rear posts. (Depending on the size of scroll you are using, you may want to make this higher or lower.) Clamp the rear posts to the work surface, and align the cross and side piece assembly with the 2" marks. Weld into place.

5. Weld this assembly to the back of the scrolls, making sure the side pieces are level.

Attach the Bobeches

1. Cut the front (C), middle (D), and rear (E) extenders to size.

2. Weld the front extenders to the tops of the scrolls. Center the rear extender over the rear crosspiece and weld in place. Set the middle extenders 4" from each end of the middle cross piece and weld in place (see photo).

3. Center a bobeche (I) over each extender, rear post, and center post. Make sure the bobeches are level, and weld in place. You may need to grind down the tops of the posts to get a level seating for the bobeches.

4. Wire brush, clean, and apply the finish of your choice.

Weld the extenders into place.

FURNITURE PROJECTS

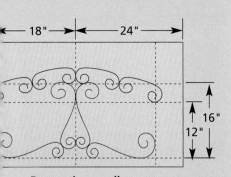

18" ← → 24"

16"
12"

**Decorative scroll
layout detail**

**Overall dimensions
36 × 10 × 56"**

Baker's Shelves

Baker's shelves are a great welding project—the possibilities are nearly endless. Many gift and furnishing stores sell various baker's shelves, but if you look closely, many have sloppy welds and thin wire scrolls. On our project, the shelves feature ¼" round bar scrolls and a nice zigzag trim. You can make the scrolls with the homemade jigs featured on page 19, which works nicely. We also tried out a scroll making attachment for a hand-powered metal bender. This scroller was meant to use flat bar stock, but by grinding the round bar ends slightly, we could bend round stock. The ground ends actually added a nice touch to the scrolls. The metal bender could be used for the zigzag as well.

PART	NAME	DIMENSIONS	QUANTITY
A	C scrolls	¼" round bar × 26½"	4
B	Top S scrolls	¼" round bar × 35"	4
C	Side S scrolls	¼" round bar × 24½"	8
D	Back legs	¾" round tube × 44"	2
E	Front legs	¾" round tube × 36"	2
F	Shelf supports, front & back	½" round tube × 34½"	8
G	Shelf supports, sides	½" round tube × 8½"	8
H	Zig zag trim	¼" round bar × 48"	4
I	Finials	1" brass or wood ball	2

MATERIALS

- ¼" round bar (54 feet)
- 16 gauge × ¾" round tube (13½ feet)
- 16 gauge × ½" round tube (29 feet)
- 4 × 6 foot plywood
- 2 × 4 foot plywood
- 1 × 2 lumber × 36" (7)
- Drywall screws
- 2 × 2 lumber × 36"
- Pre-drilled ¾" on center flat bar (3 feet)
- $\frac{5}{16}$ × 2½" machine bolts (24)
- ¾" rubber pipe tips or glides (4)
- Brass or wood finials (2)
- Tempered glass shelves cut to fit (4)

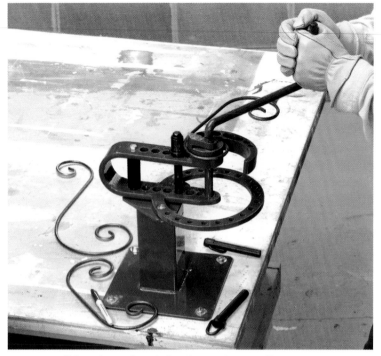

Use a scroll bender to bend the decorative scrolls.

How to Build Baker's Shelves

Prepare the Scrolls

1. Cut the C scrolls (A) and top S scrolls (B) to size.

2. Mark a stop point 10¾" from each end of a C scroll. Insert one end into the scroll maker (flatten the end by grinding, if necessary), and bend it to the stop point. Do the same for the other end (see photo, left).

3. Repeat step 2 to shape the remaining three C scrolls.

4. Mark a stop point 20" from one end of a top S scroll. Mark a stop point 8" from the other end.

5. Insert the 20" end of the S scroll into the scroll maker and bend to the stop point for the large circle. Insert the opposite end into the scroll maker and bend to the 8" mark for the small circle.

6. Repeat steps 4 to 5 to shape the other S scrolls.

Assemble the Scrolls

1. On a 2 × 4 foot sheet of plywood, lay out the scroll pattern shown below.

2. Draw a line 6" in from one side of the plywood. Draw parallel lines at 18" and 36" from this line to mark the outside edges of the back legs and the center line. Draw a perpendicular line across the bottom of these lines for the base line.

3. On the center line, mark a point 16" up from the baseline to mark the base of the uppermost C scroll pair. On the side lines, mark points 12" up from the baseline to mark the base of the side C scrolls. The back legs will meet the C scrolls at the underside of the scroll. The S scroll will butt up against the back leg. (Because the scrolls you turn will be slightly smaller or larger, you may need to adjust the layout dimensions as you go.)

4. Lay out the scrolls on the pattern. When you are satisfied with the layout of the scrolls, weld them together at the contact points.

Create the Assembly Jig

1. Use drywall screws to fasten a 3-foot piece of 1 × 2 along the long edge of a 4 × 6 piece of plywood. Attach another 3-foot piece of 1 × 2 parallel to the first piece, 36" apart. These mark the outside edges of the legs.

2. Attach a third piece of 1 × 2 across the bottom of these two, making sure the corners are square. This will align the bottom of the legs.

Lay out the scroll design dimensions on a piece of plywood. Place the scrolls into the layout, and weld at each contact point.

3. Attach four 24" pieces of 1 × 2 perpendicular to the sides at 3", 13", 23" and 33" to mark the shelf heights. Center these pieces between the side pieces.

Assemble the Legs & Shelf Supports

1. Cut the back legs (D), front legs (E), and shelf supports (F & G) to size. Grind the ends of the shelf supports slightly to fit around the curve of the legs.

2. Clamp the back legs to the side 1 × 2s, making sure the leg ends are firmly against the bottom crosspiece.

3. Clamp the back shelf supports to the four shelf crosspieces of the jig.

4. Weld the back shelf supports to the back legs.

5. Repeat steps 2 to 4 to attach the front legs to the front shelf supports.

Attach the Shelf Sides

1. Stand the back legs and shelf support assembly upright. Use a magnetic clamp to hold a shelf side support even with a back shelf support. Tack weld into place.

2. Stand the front legs and shelf support assembly upright. Align with the back assembly, and tack weld the shelf side support even with its corresponding front shelf support.

3. Continue to line up and attach the shelf side supports.

4. Place the shelf assembly on its back, and align it with the scroll assembly. Weld the two assemblies together at all contact points.

Install the ZigZag Trim

1. Cut the zigzag blanks (H) to length.

2. Bend the zigzag trim to shape. Create a bending jig by attaching a 3-foot length of pre-drilled flat bar to a 3-foot length of 2 × 2. Drill 1" deep holes through every other hole. Use 2½" bolts as the bending posts. Insert two bolts into the jig, and clamp the zigzag blank between them. Bend the metal around the second bolt and insert a third bolt, bend the metal around that, and continue (see photo, right). As you get toward the end, if you need more leverage, slip a piece of ½" tube over the rod.

3. Cut the zigzag trim to fit between the front legs.

4. Weld the zigzag trim to the legs and to points on the underside of each shelf.

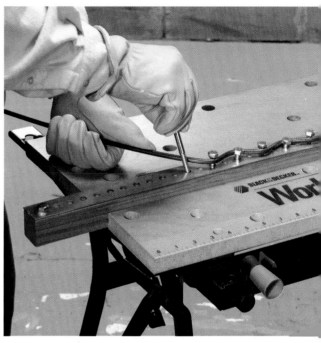

Use pre-drilled ¾" on center flat bar attached to a 2 × 2 to create a bending jig for the zig zag trim. Clamp the rod between the first two bolts and bend. Continue adding bolts and bending until complete.

Attach the Side S Scroll

1. Cut the side S scrolls (C) to size.

2. Mark a stop point 11⅞" from one end for the large circle of the scroll, and 6⅜" from the opposite end for the small circle. Do this for each S scroll.

3. Bend the scrolls at the marks.

4. Place the scrolls between the front and back legs, setting the scrolls ½" above the shelf supports to allow room for the glass shelf.

5. Weld the scrolls to the front and back legs.

Add Finishing Touches

1. Grind down all welds and spatter. Clean and wire brush or sandblast the baker's shelves. Apply the finish of your choice.

2. Install glides or rubber tips on the legs. Place finials on the front leg tops.

3. Measure the shelf dimensions, including the cutout dimensions to fit around the legs, and order tempered glass shelves cut to fit.

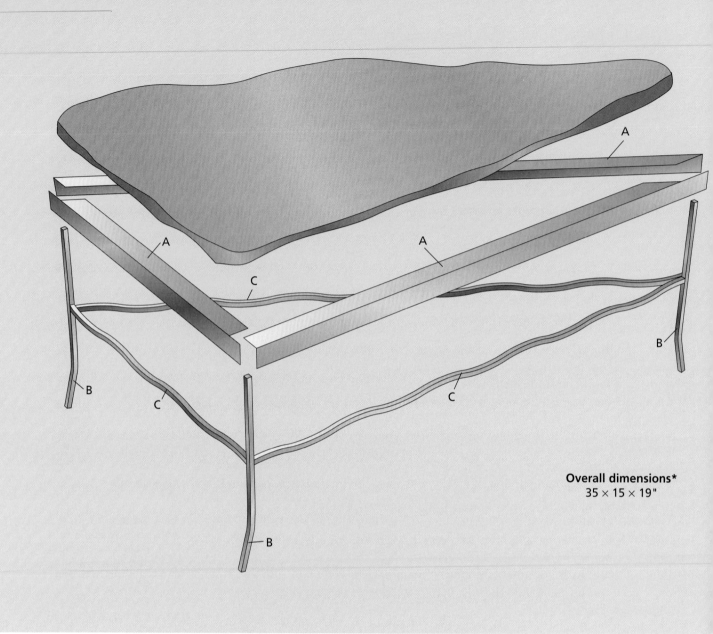

Overall dimensions*
35 × 15 × 19"

Coffee Table

A nice slab of stone or a cross section of a tree makes an appealing coffee table, but how do you support it simply and easily? A table base welded from 1" angle iron and ½" square bar can support the weight of stone or wood without being cumbersome or bulky. This design is for a triangular base to suit the piece of marble being used. Creating a layout with tape allows you to experiment with different sizes and locations for your triangle. If you are using fence pickets, as we have here, make sure the length of the longest side of the triangle does not exceed the length of the picket. Pickets are generally 35 to 39" long.

PART	NAME	DIMENSIONS	QUANTITY
A	Top supports	⅛ × 1 × 1" angle iron*	3
B	Legs	½" square bar × 20"	3
C	Wavy crosspieces	½" wavy bar fence pickets*	3

*Side pieces and top supports must be cut to fit the particular tabletop.

MATERIALS

- ⅛" × 1 × 1" angle iron (amount will vary)
- ½" square bar (5 feet)
- ½" wavy bar fence pickets (3)
- Construction adhesive, silicone glue, or screws
- Masking tape
- Table top

How to Build a Coffee Table

Create the Triangle

1. Turn the table top upside down, and use masking tape to lay out a triangle. The triangle should be at least 3" in from the edges of the table top material, but not so far in that the table will tip easily.

2. Measure each side of the triangle. Cut the top support pieces (A) to match these three measurements. Miter both ends of the longest piece.

3. Place the longest support piece on top of the second longest support. Set both pieces on the tape layout on the table top. Mark the angle and notch on the second support where it intersects the first support (see photo) to allow these pieces to butt together. Cut out the notch and angle on the support.

4. Place the two supports back together on the triangle layout. Set the third support on the layout under the first two support pieces. Mark the notches and angles at the intersections. Cut the third support piece. (You may need to make an additional angle cut on the second long piece, depending on the triangle.)

5. On a work surface, arrange the support pieces to form the triangle. Weld the outside corners. Turn the assembly over and weld the top butt joints.

6. Use an angle grinder to smooth the top joints so the table top rests on a flat surface.

Install the Legs

1. Cut the legs (B) to size.

2. Mark each leg 4" from one end. Place a leg in a bench vise, lining up the mark with the edge of the vise jaws, and bend the leg end 15°. Repeat this process for the other two legs.

3. Turn the top assembly upside down on your work surface. Place a leg in a corner with the bend of the leg pointing outward in the same line as the point of the triangle.

4. Check to make sure the leg is perpendicular to the top assembly, then tack weld in place. Tack weld the other two legs in the remaining corners the same way.

Attach the Side Pieces

1. Measure the distance between the legs. Cut one wavy crosspiece (C) to fit each of the three sides. Bevel the ends to fit the angled legs.

2. Clamp a crosspiece against two legs, 7" from the top assembly. Check for square and tack weld. Install the remaining crosspieces the same way.

3. Turn the assembly right side up and check for square and level. Make adjustments if necessary. Complete all the welds.

Complete the Table

1. Grind down the welds, if desired. (You may also want to grind down the feet of the table so they make flat contact with the floor.) Clean or wire brush the assembly. Apply your choice of finish.

2. Drill holes in the angle iron and attach a wooden table top with screws, or use silicone or construction adhesive to attach a stone top.

Place the mitered long support piece on top of the second longest support piece. Mark the angle and notch needed to fit the pieces together.

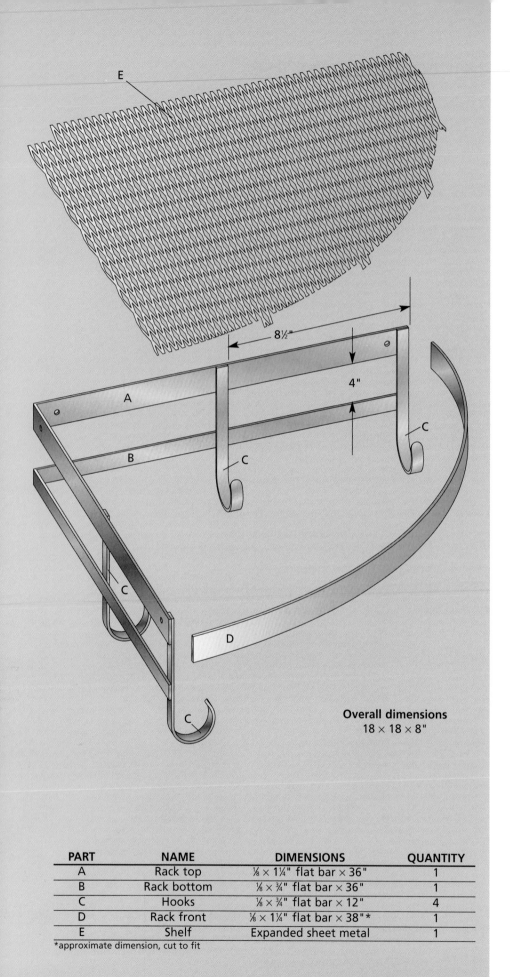

E

8½"

4"

A

B

C

C

C

D

C

Overall dimensions
18 × 18 × 8"

Corner Coatrack

In a small hallway with limited or no closet space, a corner coatrack is one of the handiest things you can add. The expanded sheet metal used for the shelf is available in a variety of thicknesses and hole sizes. You may choose to use patterned sheet metal, which is available in many designs and gauges—see the Resources section on page 140. If the shelf will be used for items heavier than hats and mittens, you will need to use thicker gauge sheet metal or add some crosspieces for support. The mounting holes are spaced to account for 16" on-center studs. If you know where you will be hanging your coatrack, locate the studs and space the mounting holes accordingly.

PART	NAME	DIMENSIONS	QUANTITY
A	Rack top	⅛ × 1¼" flat bar × 36"	1
B	Rack bottom	⅛ × ¾" flat bar × 36"	1
C	Hooks	⅛ × ¾" flat bar × 12"	4
D	Rack front	⅛ × 1¼" flat bar × 38"*	1
E	Shelf	Expanded sheet metal	1

*approximate dimension, cut to fit

MATERIALS

- ⅛ × 1¼" flat bar (7 feet)
- ⅛ × ¾" flat bar (7 feet)
- Expanded sheet metal (2 × 2 feet)
- 2" pipe
- Hanging hardware

Prepare the Rack Top & Bottom

The bend in the rack top and rack bottom takes ¼" of material. By bending the pieces at the 17¾" mark, both legs will be equal length.

1. Cut the rack top (A) and rack bottom (B) to size.

2. Drill ¼" holes in the top piece at 1", 17", 19", and 35". (These are the rack mounting holes.)

3. Mark the top piece 17¾" from one end. Place the piece in a bench vise with the mark at the edge of the vise and the longer end extending upward. Bend the end to 90°.

4. Repeat step 3 with the rack bottom piece.

Assemble the Rack

1. Cut the hooks (C) to size.

2. Grind one end of each hook into a smooth, rounded semi-circle. Make a 2"-radius bend in the rounded ends by clamping them to a section of 2" pipe and bending the hooks.

3. Lay the rack top and rack bottom on one side on your work surface, keeping them 4" apart. Make sure the ends are aligned and the bars are parallel.

4. Place a coat hook over the rack top and bottom, flush with the ends and with the top of the rack. Make sure the corners are square, then clamp the workpieces in place. Tack weld the coat hook to each bar.

5. Place the second hook 8½" from the outside edge of the first hook. Check for square, clamp in place, and tack weld to each bar.

6. Rotate the rack so the other side is flat on the work surface. Repeat steps 4 to 5 to attach the hooks to that side.

7. Make sure that all hooks are still square to the rack. Weld the hooks to each bar, starting on the side opposite the tack.

Attach the Rack Front

1. Bend the rack front (D) into an 18"-radius arc. (The easiest way to do this is to place the bar over a table edge and make a slight bend every 2" along the length of the bar. Keep making bends until the proper radius is formed.)

2. Place one end of the arc against an end of the rack top. Make a mark where the other end of the arc meets the other end of the rack top. Cut the arc to size.

3. Place the arc against the rack top, leaving an open corner for the weld. Tack weld in place.

4. Position the other end of the arc against the opposite end of the rack top. Tack weld in place. Make sure the arc is aligned properly and not twisted. Complete the corner welds.

Attach the Shelf & Finish

1. Place the rack upside down on top of the decorative sheet metal (E), with the 90° corner of the assembly 1" from the corner of the sheet metal. Using a permanent marker, trace the inside of the arc onto the sheet metal. Draw ½" tabs at regular intervals in front of the arc (see photo). Trace along the sides of the rack so you will know where to bend the sides.

2. Cut the sheet metal with a plasma cutter, tin snips, or a jig saw with a bi-metal blade. Cut a notch at the 90° corner so the sides can be bent. Bend the front tabs and sides to 90°.

3. With the rack upside down, place the shelf inside the rack so the top is flush with the top of the rack. Clamp it in place and weld the sheet metal to the rack.

4. Clean and finish the rack as desired.

Mark the ½" tabs at regular intervals on the outside.

Overall dimensions
26 × 12 × 36"

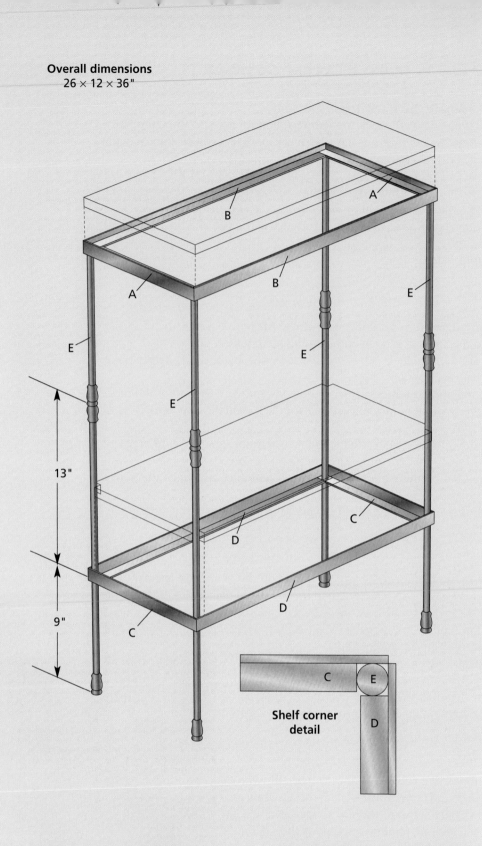

Shelf corner detail

Kitchen Appliance Stand

This freestanding table is sized to be placed next to a stove, but it could go anywhere in the house as an incidental table or plant stand.

The stand is lightweight and easy to move, yet sturdy enough to support a good deal of weight. The decorative bushings and feet provide a touch of elegance and give the stand decorative appeal.

MATERIALS

- ⅛ × 1 × 1" T-bar (6½ feet)
- ⅛ × 1 × 1" angle iron (6½ feet)
- ½" round bar (12 feet)
- Decorative bushings (4)
- Decorative feet (4)
- Ceramic tile or wood top
- Ceramic tile or wood shelf
- Felt bumpers (4)

PART	NAME	DIMENSIONS	QUANTITY
A	Top sides	⅛ × 1 × 1" T-bar × 12"	2
B	Top front and back	⅛ × 1 × 1" T-bar × 26"	2
C	Shelf sides	⅛ × 1 × 1" angle iron × 12"	2
D	Shelf front and back	⅛ × 1 × 1" angle iron × 26"	2
E	Legs	½" round bar × 36"	4

How to Build a Kitchen Appliance Stand

Build the Top
1. Cut the top sides (A) and the top front and back (B) to size. Rather than mitering the corners, cut a 1" notch at each end of the front and back pieces.
2. Position the top front and a side piece at a right angle. (Because the T-bars do not sit flat on the table top, it can be difficult to assemble the top pieces. Use shims or create a wooden clamping jig to hold the pieces securely while you align them.)
3. Check the top front and side piece for square and tack weld the corner.
4. Place the top back and other side piece together at a right angle. Check the corner for square and tack weld.
5. Assemble the two pieces to make a rectangle. Check for square by measuring diagonally between the corners. If the measurements are equal, the assembly is square. If it is not square, adjust until both measurements are equal.
6. Tack weld the top pieces together. Recheck the assembly for square, then finish the corner welds.

Build the Shelf
1. Cut the shelf sides (C) and the shelf front and back (D) to size.
2. Cut a ½" notch at both ends of all four shelf pieces to create a hole for the legs to fit through (see Shelf Corner Detail, opposite page).
3. Position the shelf front and a shelf side piece at a right angle. Check the pieces for square and tack weld the corner.
4. Repeat step 3 to weld the shelf back to the other shelf side piece.
5. Assemble the two pieces to make a rectangle. Check the assembly for square and tack weld together.
6. Recheck the assembly for square, then finish the corner welds.

Attach the Legs
1. Cut the legs (E) to size.
2. Insert the legs through the cutouts in the shelf. If using decorative slide-on bushings, position them on the legs and tack weld in place.
3. Place the top over the legs. Make sure the legs are flush against the T-bar and tack weld in place.
4. Measure 9" from the bottom of the legs and make a mark. Align the shelf with the marks and tack weld in place.
5. Stand the unit upright. Check the top and shelf for level. If they are not level, break the tack welds and adjust until level. Complete the welds between the legs and the top, and the legs and the shelf.

Attach the Feet & Finish
1. Weld, braze, or braze weld the feet in place (see photo).
2. Wire brush or sandblast the appliance stand and apply the finish of your choice.
3. Attach felt bumpers to the feet.
4. Make shelves of wood, stone, or ceramic tile, and place them on the shelf and the top.

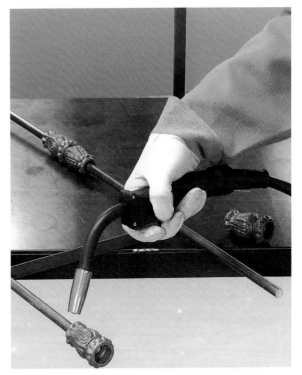

Weld around the joint between the decorative feet and the leg.

Overall dimensions
13 × 2 × 42"

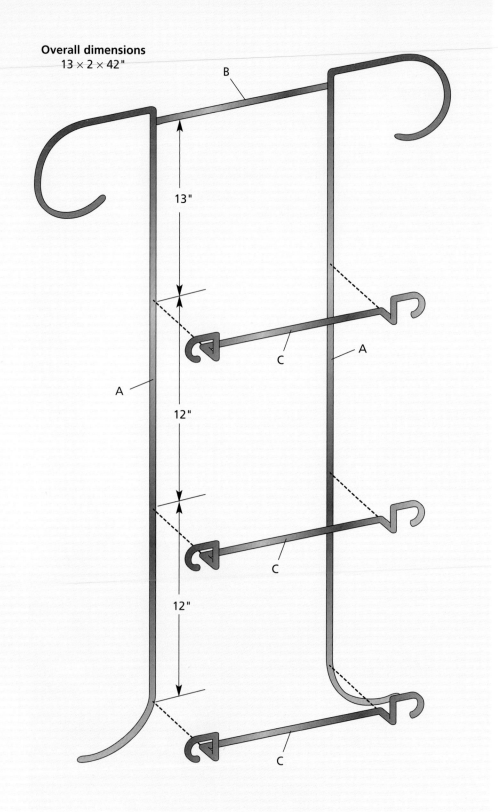

13"

12"

12"

B

A

A

C

C

C

Wall Hung Plate Rack

This rack offers a nice way to display plates and makes a great gift for a plate collector. You can use any variety of bends and scrolls to add detail to the rack. The only difficult part is the three dimensional aspect of the racks—it can be hard to follow the bend direction. You may want to adjust the spacing or the number of plate racks to fit the plates to be displayed. These directions assume a 10" diameter plate.

PART	NAME	DIMENSIONS	QUANTITY
A	Side supports	³⁄₁₆" round rod × 48"	2
B	Top piece	³⁄₁₆" round rod × 6¼"	1
C	Racks	³⁄₁₆" round rod × 16½"	3

MATERIALS

- ³⁄₁₆" round rod (13 feet)
- ½" and 3" pipe for bending jig

How to Make a Plate Rack

Prepare the Side Supports

1. Cut the side supports (A) to size.
2. Using the bending methods on page 19, make a 3" radius half circle at one end of each side support.
3. At the other end of the supports, make a 90° bend 6" from the end. Curl these ends into a 3" radius half circle. Make sure your work piece does not twist.

Prepare the Racks

1. Cut the racks (C) to size.
2. Make marks at 2", 4", and 5" from each end of the racks for bending points.
3. Bend a ½" radius curve at the first mark on each end of the racks.
4. Make a 90° bend at each of the other marks using a bench vise and ball peen hammer (see photo). Refer to the diagram on the opposite page for the orientation of the bends.

Assemble the Structure

1. Cut the top piece (B) to size.
2. Make a mark 1" down from the top of the two side supports.
3. Weld the top piece to the side supports at the 1" marks.
4. Place the first plate rack 3" from the bottom of the side supports. Square the rack to the sides and weld in place.
5. Set the remaining racks at 12" and 24" from the bottom rack. Make sure the racks are square to the sides, then weld in place.
6. Turn the rack over and weld the back side of each joint.

Apply Finishing Touches

1. Clean the structure with a wire brush.
2. Apply your choice of finish to the rack.

Make the right angle bends using a bench vise and a ball peen hammer.

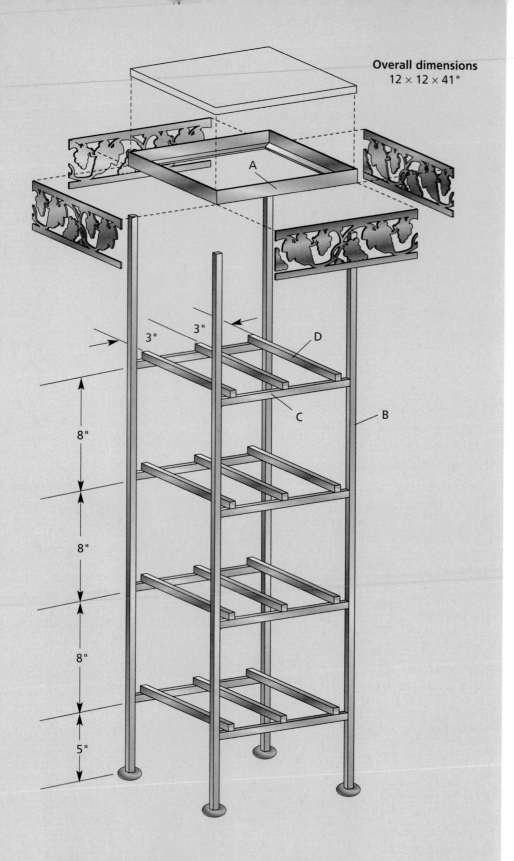

Overall dimensions
12 × 12 × 41"

3"

3"

D

C

B

A

8"

8"

8"

5"

Wine Rack

This wine rack is designed so you can install a wall or floor tile as the top surface. Measure the tile and cut the top pieces to fit. Butcher block or marble would also make a nice looking top. The decorative frieze stamping and squashed ball are available from Architectural Iron Designs—see Resources on page 140.

PART	NAME	DIMENSIONS	QUANTITY
A	Top	⅛ × 1 × 1" angle iron × 12"*	4
B	Legs	½" square bar × 40"	4
C	Rack supports	½" square bar × 11" *	8
D	Bottle holders	½" square bar × 12" *	12

*Cut to fit selected tile top

MATERIALS

- ⅛ × 1 × 1" angle iron (4½ feet)
- ½" square bar (33 feet)
- Decorative frieze (4½ feet)
- 2" Squashed balls (4)
- 12" floor or wall tile (1)

How to Make a Wine Rack

Assemble the Top

1. Cut the top pieces (A) to size to fit your top surface, mitering the corners at 45°.

2. Clamp two top pieces together with a corner clamp. Use a carpenter's square to check the pieces for square, and tack weld.

3. Repeat step 2 to assemble the other two top pieces.

4. Clamp the two L-shaped top pieces together, and check for square by measuring across both diagonals. If the measurements are equal, the assembly is square. If it is not square, adjust until both measurements are equal.

5. Tack weld the two corners. Unclamp the pieces and recheck for square. Finish welding the corner joints.

Assemble the Stand

1. Cut the legs (B), rack supports (C), and bottle holders (D) to size.

2. Mark the legs at 5", 13", 21", and 29" from one end. Mark the rack supports at 2½", 5½" and 8½" from one end.

3. Position four rack supports between two of the legs at the marks. Check the pieces for square and tack weld in place.

4. Repeat step 3 to tack weld the remaining four rack supports to the other two legs.

5. Stand the leg assemblies upright and clamp a bottle holder centered on the 5½" mark on the bottom rack support. Clamp the other end of the bottle holder to the other leg assembly. Check for square and tack weld the bottle holder in place.

6. Repeat step 5 to attach a bottle holder at the 5½" marks on the other three rack supports (see photo).

7. Make sure the legs assemblies and bottle holders are square, then add the remaining bottle holders at the 2½" and 8½" marks. Finish all welds.

Attach the Top, Legs, & Frieze

1. Place the top onto the legs and weld in place.

2. Center a squashed ball at the bottom end of each leg and weld in place.

3. Bend or cut the decorative frieze to fit around the top of the legs and top. Braze, braze weld, or tack weld the frieze into place at the top of the legs and slightly below the top.

4. Grind down the welds as needed. Wire brush or sandblast the wine rack, then apply the finish of your choice.

5. Place the tile into the top.

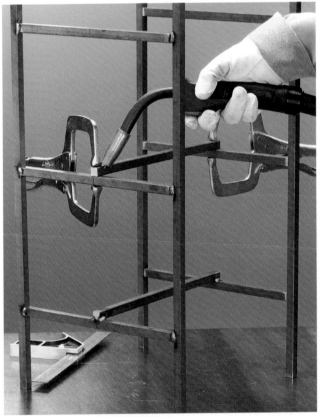

Clamp the center bottle holders to the leg assemblies and tack weld in place.

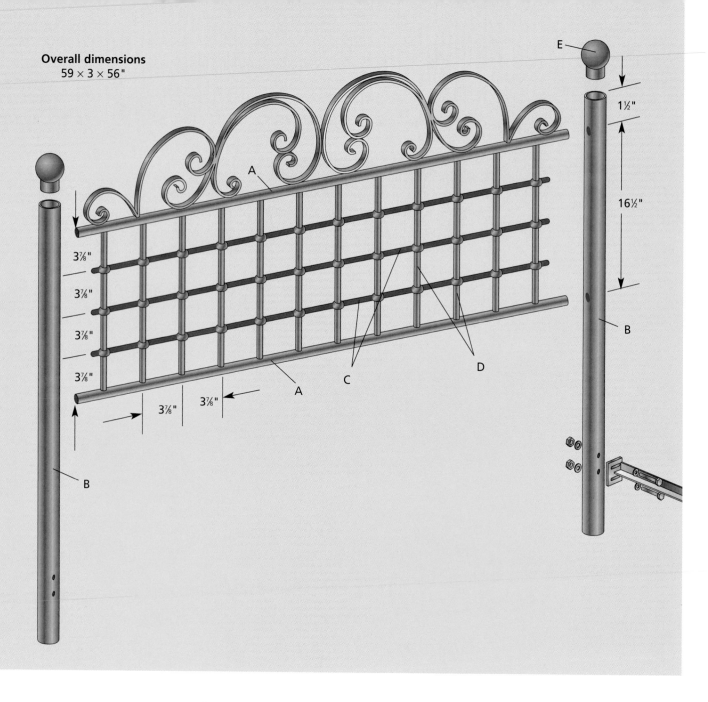

E

1½"

16½"

B

3⅞"

3⅞"

3⅞"

3⅞"

A

A

C

D

B

3⅞"   3⅞"

Headboard

A custom headboard for your bed is a great welding project. Here's an example using decorative fence and gate materials. We used top scrolls numbered 31/3 and 31/2 from Architectural Iron Designs, and hot pierced bar number SF 422US and hammered bar SF 5995 from Triple-S Steel Supply. (See Resources on page 140.)

PART	NAME	DIMENSIONS	QUANTITY
A	Top & bottom bars	⅛ × 1" round tube × 57"	2
B	End posts	⅛ × 2¼" round tube × 48"	2
C	Horizontal inserts	⅝ × 3⅞" on center decorative pierced bar × 51½"	3
D	Vertical inserts	⅝" hammered bar style rod × 18"	12
E	Finials/caps		2

How to Build a Headboard

Assemble the Grid

1. Cut the top and bottom bars (A) and end posts (B) to size.

2. Cut the horizontal inserts (C) to size, cutting at the outside edge of the pierced circle at each end. Cut the vertical inserts (D) to size.

3. Insert the vertical inserts through the holes in the horizontal inserts. Adjust the inserts so they are square.

4. Mark the top and bottom bars 3½" from each end. Align the first and last vertical inserts with the marks. Tack weld the end inserts to the bars.

5. Check the assembly for square by measuring the diagonals. If the diagonal measurements are equal, the assembly is square. Weld each vertical insert to the top and bottom bars.

6. Adjust the horizontal inserts so they are spaced evenly. Weld them to the vertical inserts at each end and at one or two points in the middle.

Insert the Grid into the End Posts

1. Place an end post in a piece of channel or angle iron and mark a straight line down the side of the post. Mark a point 1½" down from the top of the post and centered on this line.

2. Cut a 1" diameter hole centered at the mark, using a hole saw with a bi-metal blade or a plasma or flame cutter.

3. Align the top bar with the hole in the end post. Mark the placement of the hole for the bottom bar, also centered along the same line on the end post. Cut the hole in the post.

4. Repeat steps 1 to 3 to cut holes in the second end post.

5. Insert both ends of the grid assembly into the holes in the end posts (see photo). The distance between the posts should be 55". Make sure the cross bars are square to the end posts, then weld in place.

Attach Decorative Scrolls

1. Place the decorative scrolls on top of the top bar, centering them between the end posts. Weld the scrolls in place.

2. Set the post caps on top of the end posts and weld in place.

3. Wire brush or sandblast the headboard clean. Finish with your choice of finish.

4. Mark the location of the bedframe bolt holes onto the end posts. Drill ⅜" holes through the end posts. Attach the bedframe to the posts with ⅜ × 2¾" machine bolts.

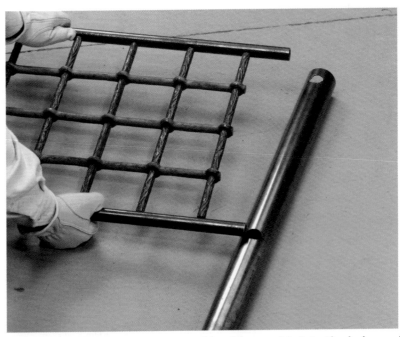

Cut holes in the end posts. Insert the grid assembly into the holes and weld in place.

OUTDOOR PROJECTS

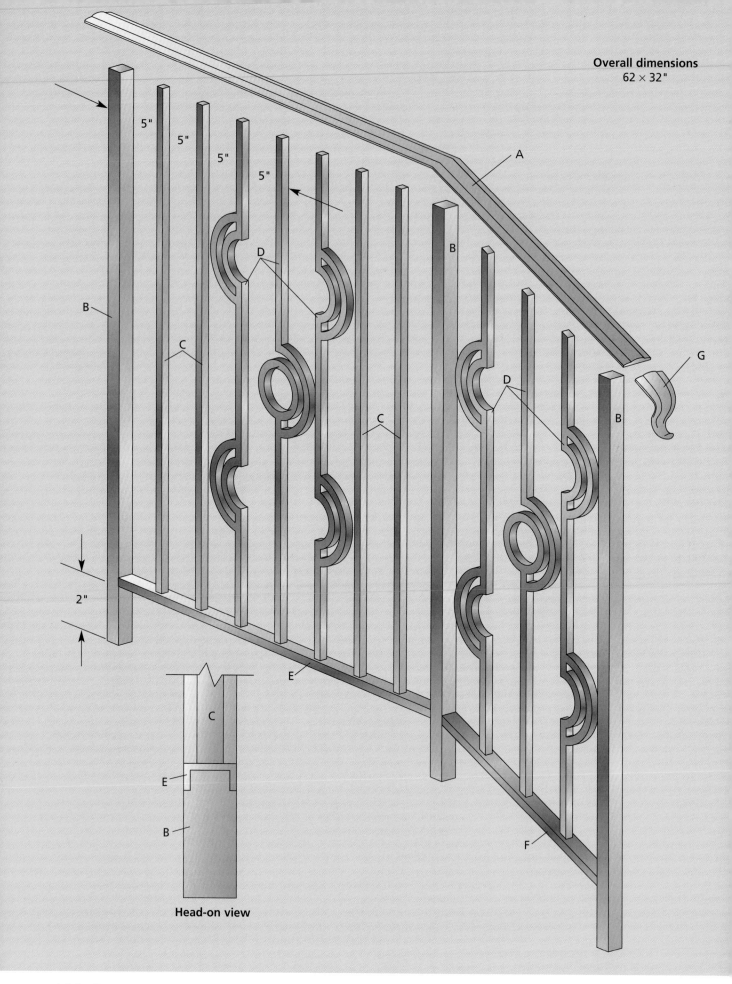

Overall dimensions
62 × 32"

A

5"

5"

5"

5"

B

B

B

B

C

C

D

D

E

F

G

2"

Head-on view

C

E

B

Stair Railing

With the number of companies selling decorative metal pickets and newel posts, it is easy to create a railing distinctly your own. The railing we are making is for a two step concrete stairway.

Some important information about creating railings:

The rail top should not be interrupted by knobs or other decorations—it must allow continuous hand to rail contact and should be between 1½" and 2" in diameter to ensure easy gripping.

Some railings—like one that is mounted against a wall or in an area where the stair surface is not raised above the surrounding surface, like the stairs in the slope of your lawn—can be a single rail at the appropriate height. A railing that separates the stair, landing, balcony, or deck from a vertical drop has to conform to certain safety standards. The pickets or balusters must not have any gaps larger than 5½" to prevent children from poking their heads through and getting stuck. The lower rail should not be more than 2 inches from the floor surface. If the vertical drop from the floor line is more than 6 feet, the railing must be a minimum of 34" tall. If the vertical drop is less than 6 feet, the railing must be a minimum of 32" in height. Railings must have turn-outs or roundovers at their ends to prevent blunt projections. The safest handrails continue 12" beyond the top and bottom stairs. Railings must be able to withstand a 250 pound force in any direction without giving way.

You can purchase rail cap, also called cap rail or handrail, at most steel supply centers. Handrail terminations come in a variety of styles. Those that scroll in an S shape are called "lamb tongues." A volute is a spiral termination, and a lateral is a flat curl to the side. These may be ordered through specialty railing distributors. (See Resources page 140.)

(See Resources page 140.)

MATERIALS

- 1¾" rail cap (as needed)
- 1" square tube (as needed)
- ½" square rod (as needed)
- ½" decorative pickets (as needed)
- ⅛ × ½ × 1" channel (as needed)
- Lamb tongue rail termination
- Mounting hardware

PART	NAME	DIMENSIONS	QUANTITY
A	Handrail	1¾" rail cap × 64"*	1
B	Newel posts	⅛ × 1 × 1" square tube × 36"	3*
C	Plain pickets	½" square rod × 30"	4*
D	Decorative pickets	½" decorative pickets × 30"	6*
E	Flat bottom rail	⅛ × ½ × 1" channel × 40"*	1
F	Angled bottom rail	⅛ × ½ × 1" channel × 24"*	1
G	Rail termination		1

*Dimensions and quantities must be adjusted to fit the particular stairs.

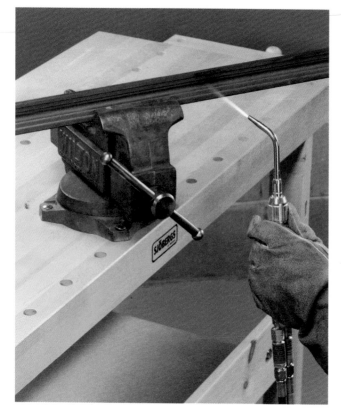

Heat the bending point of the handrail to red hot with an acetylene torch or cutting tip to make the metal easy to bend.

How to Build Stair Railing

Cut the Handrail to Length

1. Measure from the edge of the house to the edge of the landing. Measure from the edge of the landing to where the newel post will be located. Add these two measurements to get the length of the handrail.
2. Cut the handrail (A) to size.

Shape the Handrail

It is a good idea to create an angle guide for bending the handrail by screwing two pieces of wood together at the length and angle to match the stairway.
1. Set the handrail on the landing with one end butting against the house. Mark the handrail at the edge of the landing.
2. Clamp the railing in a bench vise and heat the bending point red hot with an acetylene torch (see photo, left). A cutting torch preheat works best, just make sure you don't hit the oxygen and accidentally cut the metal.
3. When the metal is red hot, bend it to create the angle. It is helpful if you pull on the longer end of the rail to bend so you have more leverage.
4. When finished bending the handrail, place it on the stairs to make sure the bend is correct.

Lay Out the Newel Posts & Pickets

The newel posts will be anchored in the concrete or attached using square footings that will bolt into the concrete, so they have to be far enough from the edge not to destroy the edge of the concrete.
1. Determine the number of plain pickets (C), decorative pickets (D), and newel posts (B) you need.
2. Place the bent handrail on the floor or a large work surface. Place newel posts at each end of the handrail and near the bend.
3. Lay out the pickets in a pleasing pattern, making sure they are no more than 5½" apart (see photo, right).
4. Mark and cut the two bottom rails (E & F) to fit between the newel posts, once you have the layout determined. Place the channel flat side up, with the legs down. Mark the picket locations on the railings.
OPTION: When you look at railings, you will see that some railings have the pickets and newel posts welded directly to the rail cap, as you see here. Other railings have a piece of channel welded into the underside of the rail cap and the pickets are welded to the flat side of the channel. Punched channel can be purchased with ½ × ½" square holes pierced through it. This is welded under the rail cap, and the pickets are inserted through the punched holes and welded in place. You also can use the punched channel for the bottom rail. Using punched channel means you cannot adjust spacing to account for the unique shapes and sizes of decorative pickets.

Cut the Posts & Pickets to Length

Purchased decorative pickets range from 36" to 39". When cutting decorative pickets, cut equal amounts from each end unless you wish the pattern to be off center.

1. Determine the height of your handrail and the depth that the newel posts will be footed in the concrete (if they are to be footed, otherwise measure to the top of the concrete).

2. Cut the newel posts and pickets to length. Cut the appropriate angle for the stair pickets.

Assemble the Railing

Concrete can explode when heated, so it is best to do your welds on a sheet of plywood that can be doused with water when you have finished.

1. Tack weld the newel posts to the rail cap. Tack weld the bottom rails to the newel posts.

2. Place the rail assembly on the stairs to make sure the dimensions are correct. If they are not, break or grind off the tack welds and make adjustments.

3. Return the assembly to the work surface, and tack weld the pickets in place, maintaining the proper spacing. Use a combination square to check each piece for square before welding.

4. Make the final welds. Weld the lamb tongue termination to the end of the rail cap.

5. Grind down any rough or unsightly welds. Wire brush or sandblast the rail assembly.

6. Install the railing by cementing the newel posts into the stairs or using bolt-down flange shoes.

7. Prime and paint the railing with a high quality outdoor metal paint.

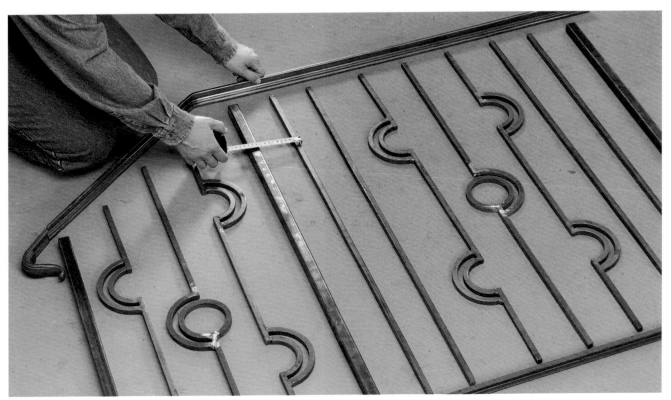

Lay out the pickets and newel posts in a pleasing arrangement, keeping them no more than 5½" apart.

Alternate styles

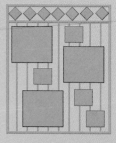

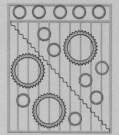

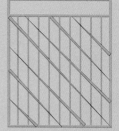

Overall dimensions
40 × 1 × 46"

Gate

This gate framework can be used to hold a collection of found metal objects. Use brazing or braze welding to join non-matching metals or thicknesses of metals. Rusty objects will need to be cleaned at the point of contact. If the objects you find are large, you may want to space the uprights at 8", rather than 4". The 4" spacing meets code requirements for gates and fences—this spacing prevents children from getting their heads stuck between uprights.

PART	NAME	DIMENSIONS	QUANTITY
A	Sides	16 gauge 1 × 1" square tube × 46"	2
B	Crosspieces	16 gauge 1 × 1" square tube × 40"	2
C	Interior crosspiece	16 gauge 1 × 1" square tube × 38"	1
D	Vertical inserts	16 gauge ½ × ½" square tube × 40"	9

How to Make a Gate

MATERIALS

- 16 gauge 1 × 1" square tube (17½ feet)
- 16 gauge ½ × ½" square tube (30 feet)
- 4" weldable barrel hinges (2)
- Gate latch hardware
- Found objects
- Wood and brass spacers

Assemble the Frame

1. Cut the sides and crosspieces (A & B) to size, mitering the ends at 45°.

2. Place the left side piece and bottom crosspiece together at a 90° angle to form one corner of the rectangle. Check the pieces for square, and clamp in place. Tack weld the pieces together.

3. Place the right side piece and top crosspiece together to form another corner of the rectangle. Check for square, clamp in place, and tack weld together.

4. Join the two pieces to form the rectangle. Check the corners for square and clamp in place. Tack weld the corners together.

5. Measure the diagonals of the rectangle to check for square. If the measurements of both diagonals are equal, the assembly is square. If it is not square, pull or push it into alignment. When aligned, clamp it in place, and finish the corner welds.

6. Turn the assembly over, and complete the welds.

Attach the Interior Crosspiece & Inserts

1. Cut the interior crosspiece (C) and vertical inserts (D) to size.

2. Place the interior crosspiece against the inside edges of the side pieces, 5" down from the top crosspiece. Check the pieces for square, and clamp in place. Weld the interior crosspiece to the sides.

3. Place the vertical inserts at 4" intervals between the interior and bottom crosspieces. Make sure the spacing is even—you might need to adjust to slightly less or more than 4" if the miter cuts are slightly off. Keep the outside edge of the inserts flush with the outside edge of the crosspieces.

4. When the spacing is adjusted properly and the inserts are square to the crosspieces, tack weld each insert at both ends.

5. Check the assembly and inserts for square one more time. Turn the assembly over, and weld each upright in place.

Attach the Found Objects

Objects other than mild steel will need to be brazed or braze welded. Connect non-metallic objects by wrapping or folding a thin strip of mild steel sheet metal or a short piece of ⅛" steel rod around an edge. Weld the ends of the rod or strap to the framework.

1. Arrange your found objects artfully across the interior space.

2. Carefully clean rust or paint from the areas where the found objects contact the uprights.

3. Weld the found objects in place.

Attach the hinges

Our gate is made to hang attached to a metal gate post. We chose to use barrel style hinges.

1. Place the gate between the gate posts. Use wood spacers and braces to position the gate between the gate posts, and clamp or brace solidly in place.

2. Line up the hinges on the post and the gate (see photo). Use a level to check for plumb. (For the gate to swing properly, the hinges need to be installed perfectly plumb.) Tack weld the hinges to the gate and post.

3. Remove the bracing, and check that gate swings freely. When it does, complete the hinge welds.

4. Install the gate latch hardware. If the hardware is painted or zinc coated, grind off the coating before welding, or install with screws.

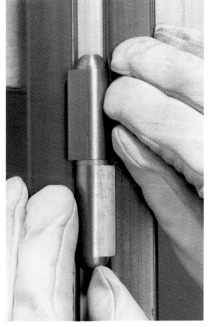

Brace the gate in position between the gate posts. Clamp a wood spacer between the gate post and the gate side. Position the hinge and check for plumb.

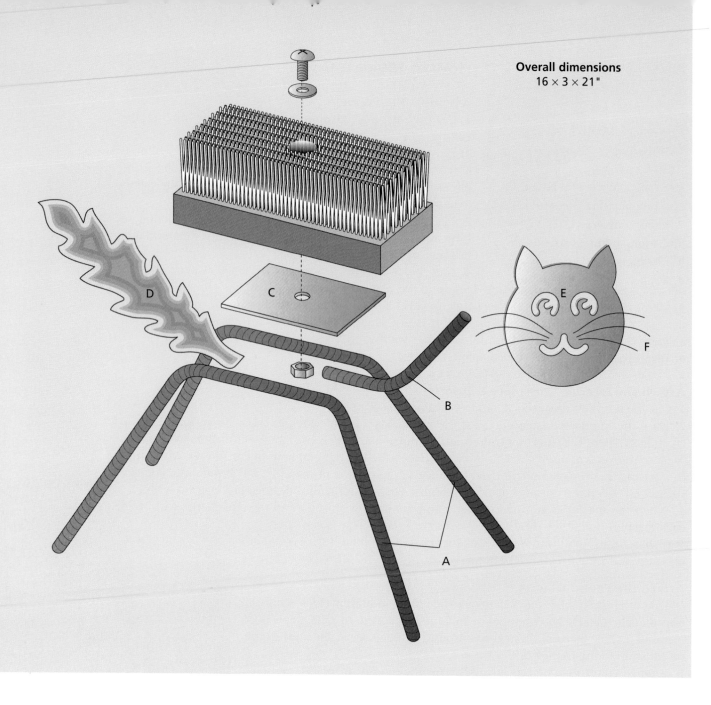

Overall dimensions
16 × 3 × 21"

Critter Boot Brush

A critter boot brush is a fun and functional addition to your back door area. This critter is made to be stuck in the ground (then the mud flies on the grass, not around the door!) but it can be mounted in cement or even on a hefty chunk of wood. This plan is for a cat because the brush mimics the classic upright fur look of an angry cat, but any animal could have this scratchy back.

PART	NAME	DIMENSIONS	QUANTITY
A	Legs	⅜ or ½" rebar × 30"	2
B	Neck	⅜ or ½" rebar × 12"	1
C	Body	⅛ or 3⁄16 × 3" flat bar × 6"	1
D	Tail	16 gauge sheet metal × 4 × 14"	1
E	Face	⅜ or ¼" plate × 5 × 5"	1
F	Whiskers	16 gauge wire × 4"	6

How to Make a
Critter Boot Brush

MATERIALS

- ⅜ or ½" rebar (6 feet)
- ⅛ or ³⁄₁₆ × 3" flat bar (6")
- 16 gauge sheet metal (4 × 14")
- ⅜ or ¼" plate (5 × 5")
- Wire or bristle brush with handle hole
- 2" machine bolt, washer, and nut
- 16 gauge wire (24")

Prepare the Legs & Neck

1. Cut the legs (A) to length.

2. Mark each leg 12" from each end. Using a bench vise, bend the legs at the marks to a 75° to 85° angle.

3. Cut the neck (B) to length.

4. Make a mark 3" from one end of the neck. Bend the neck at the mark to 85°.

Assemble the Body

1. Cut the body (C) to size.

2. Drill, flame cut, or plasma cut a hole through the center of the body for the placement of the brush.

3. Place the legs lengthwise along the edges of the body, and weld in place.

4. Position the hole in the brush over the hole in the body to get the spacing for the neck extension (if the neck is set back too far, the brush will not lay flat).

5. Weld the neck in place.

Attach the Tail

1. Use flame or plasma cutting to cut the tail (D), leaving a minimum of 4" of straight flat metal for attachment.

2. Remove any slag from the tail, and weld in place between the legs at the opposite end from the neck (see photo).

Prepare & Attach the Face

If using a flame cutter for the face, you will get the best results if you allow the metal to cool between cutting each individual feature. If you don't let it cool, the metal begins to melt and round over, making it difficult to get a sharp outline of the features.

1. Use flame or plasma cutting to cut out the face shape (E) and features.

2. Remove any slag from the back side of the face. Cut the whiskers (F) to size and attach to the face.

3. Position the face and weld it to the end of the neck.

Attach Brush & Set in Place

1. Bolt the brush onto the body and adjust the tail in an upright position.

2. Push the legs into the ground or mount the critter in a concrete base.

Cut and bend the legs and neck to size, then weld the legs, neck, and tail to the body.

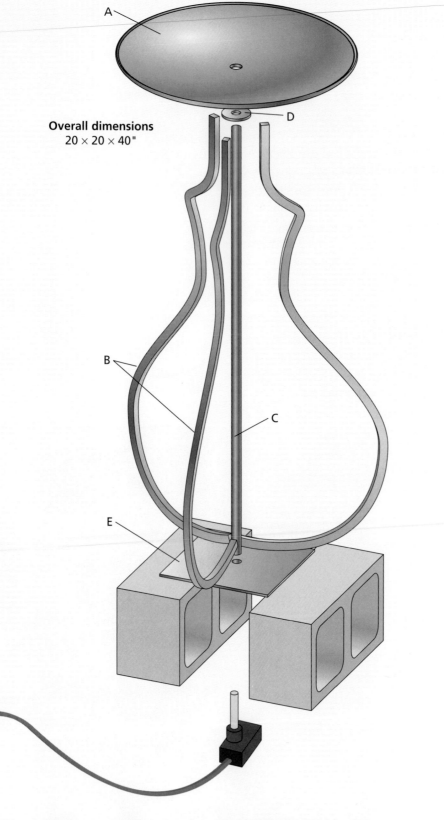

A

Overall dimensions
20 × 20 × 40"

B

C

E

D

Disk Fountain

This fountain uses a plow disk, which can be found at farm implement stores, and three decorative fence pickets. Decorative scrolls also could be used. You'll get to see how watertight your welds are, because you'll need to weld the supply pipe and a flange to the disk. You could use a slightly smaller disk for the base—we simply used a square plate.

PART	NAME	DIMENSIONS	QUANTITY
A	Basin	9 gauge × 20" plow disk	1
B	Legs	Decorative pickets × 35"	3
C	Supply pipe	1/8 × 1" round tube × 35½"	1
D	Flange	3/16" sheet metal × 3" circle	1
E	Base	1/4" plate × 12 × 12"	1

MATERIALS

- 9 gauge × 20" plow disk (1)
- Decorative fence pickets (3)
- ⅛ × 1" round tube (3 feet)
- ³⁄₁₆" sheet metal (3" circle)
- ¼" plate (12 × 12")
- Fountain and pump

How to Make a Disk Fountain

Assemble the Flange

You can purchase round metal blanks in 3" sizes, or you can cut your own. We purchased one at a steel surplus store.

1. Cut the supply pipe (C), flange (D), and base (E) to size.

2. Cut a 1" diameter hole in the center of the flange and the center of the base.

3. Place the hole in the flange over the end of the supply pipe and weld all around.

4. Grind down the weld until it is flush.

Attach the Basin

1. Grind off the paint from the basin (A) in a 4" diameter circle around the center hole.

2. Turn the basin over and place the flange and pipe assembly on top of it, centering it over the hole in the basin.

3. Tack weld the flange to the disk in at least three places. Make sure the supply pipe is perpendicular to the basin, then complete the weld all around the flange.

Attach the Legs

1. Tack weld the legs to the basin assembly (see photo), keeping an equal distance between each leg.

2. Insert the supply pipe into the hole in the base and tack in place.

3. Turn the assembly upright, and check for level. Adjust if necessary. Complete the welds for the legs and the base.

Apply Finishing Touches

1. Grind down all rough welds. Thoroughly wire brush or sandblast the fountain.

2. Prime and paint the fountain with a high quality outdoor metal paint.

3. Place the fountain on a brick or cement block base in a pool or over an appropriately sized reservoir.

4. Install the fountain hardware and tubing following manufacturer's directions.

Tack weld the pickets to the basin and to the supply tube.

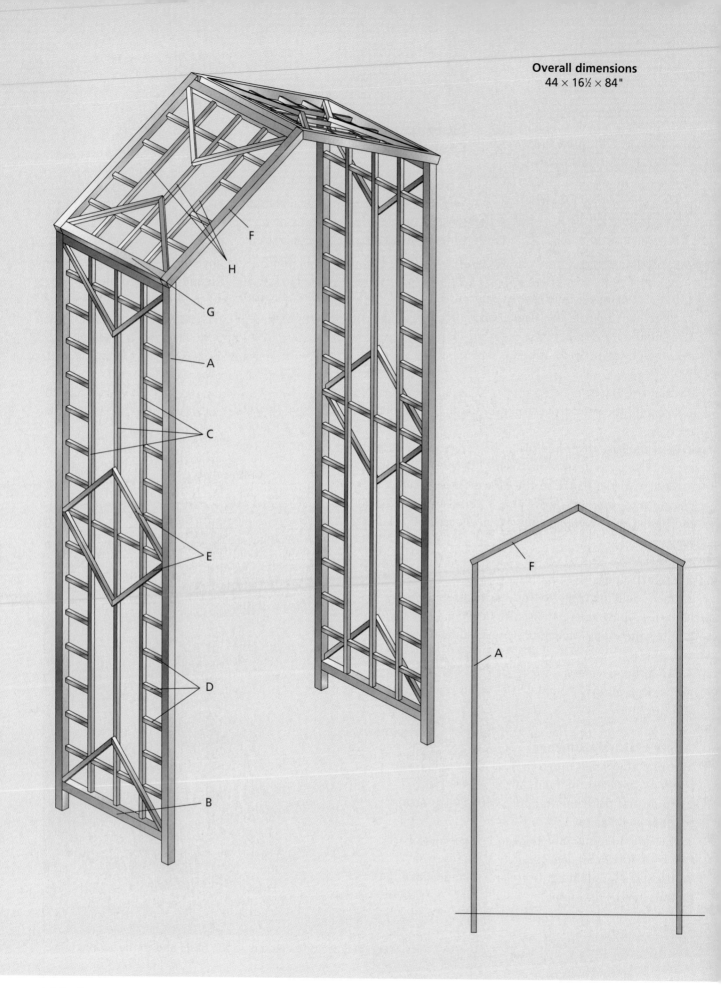

Overall dimensions
44 × 16½ × 84"

F

H

G

A

C

E

D

B

F

A

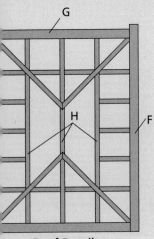

Roof Detail

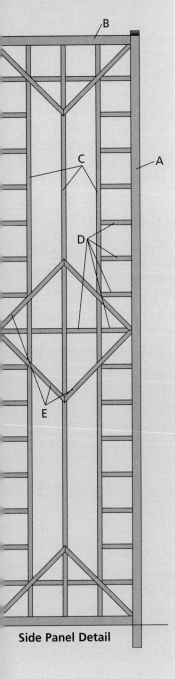

Side Panel Detail

Arbor

This distinctive arbor will add a touch of class to any garden. Modeled after the "Prairie Style," its clean lines are straightforward to cut and weld, and they provide plenty of climbing support for a variety of vines. The ½" inserts are placed flush with the back of the 1" sides and ends, eliminating the need for difficult centering and giving an increased sense of depth. The arbor can be made from the 6-foot steel lengths available at home improvement centers, but because of the amount of steel used, a trip to a steel supplier might be worthwhile, especially if you have a way to transport 20-foot lengths. The ½" square tube bows quite easily, so if you do buy 20 foot lengths, make sure they are well supported in transit. Otherwise, they will bow and not be suitable for the vertical inserts.

PART	NAME	DIMENSIONS	QUANTITY
A	Panel sides	16 gauge 1 × 1" square tube × 72"	4
B	Panel ends	16 gauge 1 × 1" square tube × 15½"	4
C	Panel vertical inserts	16 gauge ½ × ½" square tube × 63½"	6
D	Horizontal inserts	16 gauge ½ × ½" square tube × 3½"	100
E	Diagonal inserts	16 gauge ½ × ½" square tube × 12"*	24
F	Roof ends	16 gauge 1 × 1" square tube × 15½"	4
G	Roof sides	16 gauge 1 × 1" square tube × 25½"	4
H	Roof vertical inserts	16 gauge ½ × ½" square tube × 23½"	6

*Approximate dimension, cut to fit

MATERIALS

- 16 gauge 1 × 1" square tube (44 feet)
- 16 gauge ½ × ½" square tube (100 feet)
- Wood scraps

Check the panel for square by measuring the diagonals. If the measurements are equal, the assembly is square.

How to Build an Arbor

Assemble the Panels

Set up the project on a sheet of ¼" plywood placed on sawhorses. Make sure the plywood is not bowed or it will cause misalignment of the project pieces. Working on a raised surface is easier than working on the floor, and you can clamp the metal to the plywood. Remember to clamp your work cable to the workpiece. If you want the arbor wider or narrower than 44", you must adjust the miter angles for the roof and side panels.

1. Cut the panel sides (A) to size, mitering one end at 30°. The mitered end is the top. Cut the panel ends (B), vertical inserts (C), and horizontal inserts (D) to size.

2. Place a panel end between the top of two panel sides, keeping the outside edge of the panel end flush with the short ends of the mitered panel sides. Clamp the pieces in place.

3. Position three vertical inserts between the two panel sides. (This is just to hold the bottom panel end in place. The exact location of the inserts is not important at this time.)

4. Place the bottom panel end between the panel sides, keeping it snug against the vertical inserts. Clamp the bottom panel end in place.

5. Remove the vertical inserts. Use a carpenter's square to check the panel sides and ends for square. Tack weld each corner. Check for square again by measuring the two diagonals (see photo, page 135). If the measurements are equal, the panel is square. If not, adjust the workpieces until the diagonals are the same.

6. Turn the panel over and complete the welds at the four corners. Grind the tack welds flat so the panel lays flat on the work surface.

Attach the Vertical & Horizontal Inserts

1. Replace the vertical inserts between the panel sides. Place several horizontal inserts between the vertical inserts and the panel sides to ensure the correct spacing of the vertical inserts.

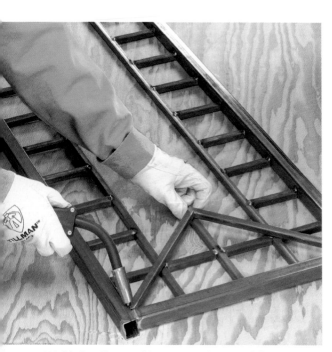

Weld the diagonal inserts to the panel framework and to the center vertical insert.

2. Weld the vertical inserts to the panel top and bottom.

3. Place the horizontal inserts into the vertical framework every 3½". (Use horizontal inserts as spacers.)

4. Starting at the top of the panel, use a combination square to align the first row of horizontal inserts. Once they are aligned, weld them in place.

5. Continue aligning and welding the inserts one row at a time. If the vertical inserts are bowed side to side, use a clamp to hold them against the inserts. If they bow upward, weight them down with a sandbag or other weight.

Insert the Diagonal Inserts

1. Cut four diagonal inserts (E) to size, mitering one end at 45°.

2. Place two diagonal inserts against the bottom edge of the top panel. The mitered ends of the inserts should butt together over the middle vertical insert. Mark the other end of the diagonal inserts where they cross the top panel so they will fit in the corner.

3. Make the angled cuts on the diagonal inserts.

4. Grind down the welds that will be underneath the diagonal inserts so they will lie flat. Weld the diagonal inserts in place (see photo, left).

5. Repeat steps 2 to 4 to weld the diagonal inserts to the bottom of the panel.

6. Cut four more diagonal inserts, mitering both ends at 45°.

7. Center these four inserts over the eighth row of horizontal inserts to form a diamond shape. Weld the inserts in place.

8. Repeat this entire process to construct a second panel.

Build the Roof Panels

1. Construct two roof panels following the same procedure used for the side panels, except there is no central diamond insert.

Make clamping blocks out of wood scraps. Clamp the roof panels to the blocks. Place two or three tack welds along the joint between the panel ends.

2. Stand the roof panels on edge and join the mitered ends to form the 120° angle for the roof peak.

3. Clamp the roof panels in place. (You may need to attach temporary wooden clamping points to the work surface by fastening 1 × 2 or 2 × 4 scraps to match the layout. Clamp the panels to the scraps.) Place two or three tack welds along the joint between the panel ends (see photo, above).

Fasten the Roof to the Sides

1. Place a side panel on edge, and set it against one side of the roof panel. Line them up so the mitered edge of the side panel is making contact with the bottom edge of the roof panel. Clamp the panels in place.

2. Tack weld the panels at two points along the joint (see photo, below).

3. Repeat steps 1 and 2 for the other side panel.

4. Measure the distance between the tops and the bottoms of the side panels to ensure the panels are an equal distance apart at both ends.

5. Check the panels for square by measuring the diagonals. Make any necessary adjustments, and make sure the roof assembly is still fitted against the side panels.

6. Weld all the mitered roof peak joints and the mitered joints between the side panels and the roof panels.

Finishing Touches

To prevent putting stress on the welds, and to maintain the arbor's shape, clamp wooden crosspieces between the panel sides before moving it.

1. The easiest finish for the arbor is to allow it to gently rust over the years. You may want to place plastic end caps over the exposed tube ends on the roof, or you can weld on small caps.

2. The arbor can sit on the ground or can be mounted in concrete footings. If you live in a windy location, you may want to drive four lengths of rebar into the ground and slip the arbor legs over them.

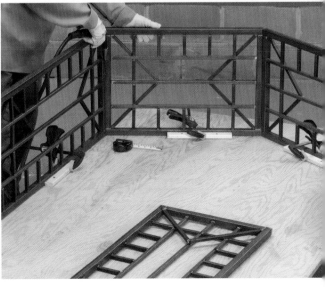

Place tack welds along the joint between the roof and side panels.

GLOSSARY

Active gas	A gas, such as oxygen, that will react with other substances.
Alloy	A substance composed of two or more metals or a metal and other non-metal material.
Arc welding	Welding processes that use an electric arc to produce heat to melt and fuse the base metals. Often used to refer specifically to shielded metal arc welding.
Backfire and flashback	Combustion taking place inside the oxyacetylene torch creating a loud pop or explosion.
Base metal	The metal that is being welded, brazed, braze welded, or cut.
Bead or weld bead	The seam between workpieces that have been joined with welding.
Braze	A process used to join metals using a non-ferrous material that melts above 850° F but below the melting point of the base metal. Brazing uses capillary action to join closely fitted parts.
Braze welding	A process used to join metals with a filler material that melts above 840° F and below the melting point of the base metal where the filler metal is not distributed by capillary action.
Butt joint	A joint between two workpieces in the same plane.
Carburizing flame	An oxyfuel flame with an excess of fuel.
Consumable electrode	An electrode that also serves as the filler material.
Corner joint	A joint between workpieces meeting at right angles and forming an L shape.
Cutting tip	Converts an oxyfuel welding torch into an oxyfuel cutting torch.
Direct current electrode negative	Direct current welding where the electrode is negative and the workpiece is positive.
Direct current electrode positive	Direct current welding where the electrode is positive and the workpiece is negative.
Duty cycle	The amount of continuous time in a 10-minute period that an arc welder can run before it needs to cool down. Expressed as a percentage at a given amperage output.
Edge joint	A joint between parallel workpieces.
Electrode	The conductive element that makes the connection with the workpiece to create an electrical arc.
FCAW	Flux cored arc welding.
Filler, filler metal	Metal added to a welded joint.
Fillet weld	A triangular shaped weld between two members that meet at 90° angles.
Flame cutting	See oxyfuel cutting.
Flux	A chemical compound that produces cleaning action and reduces the formation of oxides when heated.
Flux core, flux cored wire	An electrode for flux cored arc welding that contains flux within a wire tube.

Flux cored arc welding (FCAW)	A semi-automatic arc welding process using an electrode wire that contains flux.
Gas metal arc welding (GMAW)	A semi-automatic arc welding process using a wire electrode which also is the filler material. An inert gas is distributed over the weld area to shield the molten metal from oxygen. Commonly referred to as MIG (metal inert gas) or wire feed.
Gas tungsten arc welding (GTAW)	An arc welding process using a tungsten electrode, hand-held filler material, and an inert shielding gas. Also referred to as TIG (tungsten inert gas) and Heliarc.
GMAW	Gas metal arc welding.
Groove weld	A weld made in grooves between workpieces.
GTAW	Gas tungsten arc welding.
Heliarc	Gas tungsten arc welding.
Inert gas	A non-reactive or non-combining gas such as argon or helium.
Kerf	The width of a cut.
Lap joint	A joint between overlapping workpieces.
MIG	Metal inert gas—see gas metal arc welding.
Oxyacetylene cutting	Oxyfuel cutting using acetylene as the fuel gas.
Oxyacetylene welding	Oxyfuel welding using acetylene as the fuel gas.
Oxyfuel cutting	Cutting process using the combustion of a pressurized fuel gas and oxygen to heat steel to 1600° F at which time a pure oxygen stream is delivered to burn through the metal. Also called flame cutting.
Oxyfuel welding	Welding process that uses the heat produced by the combustion of a pressurized fuel gas and pressurized oxygen. A hand-held filler material is used. Also called gas welding.
Plasma cutting	An arc cutting process using a constricted arc. Compressed air or inert gas blows the molten metal from the kerf
Plate	Flat metal thicker than ³⁄₁₆".
Saddle joint	A joint between round tubes where one tube has been cut to fit around the other.
Sheet metal	Flat metal ³⁄₁₆" or less in thickness.
Shielded metal arc welding (SMAW)	An arc welding process using a flux coated consumable electrode. Also referred to as arc welding or stick welding.
Shielding gas	A gas that prevents contaminants from entering the molten weld pool.
Slag	Oxidized impurities formed as a coating over the weld bead; waste material found along the bottom edge of an oxyfuel cut.
SMAW	Shielded metal arc welding.
Spatter	Small droplets or balls of metal stuck to the base metal around the weld. Produced by shielded metal arc, gas metal arc, and flux cored arc welding.
Stick welding	Shielded metal arc welding.
T-joint	A joint between workpieces meeting at right angles and forming a T shape.
TIG	Tungsten inert gas—see gas tungsten arc welding.
Wire feed	See gas metal arc welding.

RESOURCES

Thanks to Tony Litwinchuk of Toll Gas & Welding Supply for arranging for the generous loan of the welding machinery pictured in this book. Thank you to Loren Johnson, also of Toll, for his technical advice on a variety of issues. Thank you to Jerry Foley and Dwight Affeldt, the welding instructors at Minneapolis Community and Technical College Continuing Eduction and Training Programs. Their knowledge of and enthusiasm for welding is fantastic. Thank you to Dwight also for reading the book and suggesting changes to make it more accurate. Finally, thank you to Paige Gamet for giving me the gift of my first welding class. —*Karen Ruth*

Architectural Iron Designs, Inc.
950 South 2nd Street
Plainfield, NJ 07063
800-784-7444
www.archirondesign.com

e-Tarps.com
1205-202 Winter Springs Court
Louisville, KY 40243
www.e-tarps.com

Garland's Inc.
2501 26th Avenue South
Minneapolis, MN 55406
800-809-7888
www.garlandsinc.com

Toll Gas & Welding Supply
3005 Niagara Lane
Plymouth, MN 55447
763-551-5300
www.tollgas.com

Triple-S Steel Supply Company
6000 Jensen Drive
Houston, TX 77026
800-392-3655
www.sss-steel.com

**Wagner Railing Systems
and Components**
J.G. Braun Company
10600 West Brown Deer Road
Milwaukee, WI 53224
800-786-2111
www.rbwagner.com
www.jgbraun.com

CONTRIBUTORS

Beateworks, Inc.
Los Angeles, CA
©Millet/Inside/Beateworks: p. 5 (top)

Birds & Beasts
rustybeast@myway.com
www.birdsandbeasts.com

ColdSnap Photography
Two Harbors, MN
©John Gregor/ColdSnap Photography: p. 4

Gene Olson
gene@mettleworks.com
Elk River, MN
Photo p. 6 (top left) by Ytsma Photography
St. Paul, MN

Heebie GBS Metalworks
www.heebiegbs.com

Lizard Breath Ranch, Inc.
Critters from the "Hood"
(free standing animals cut from
truck roofs and hoods)
www.lizardbreathranch.com
505-534-4881

Sleeper Welding
www.sleeperwelding.com
603-524-1597

INDEX